"Born to Survive"

a true-life story

by

Maureen Spelman

**Grosvenor House
Publishing Limited**

This book is published by
Grosvenor House Publishing Ltd
28-30 High Street, Guildford, Surrey, GU1 3HY.
www.grosvenorhousepublishing.co.uk

A CIP record for this book
is available from the British Library

ISBN 978-1-906645-95-3

Dedication

I dedicate this book to my family, who have loved me and stood by me through many painful times. To my loving and steadfast husband, Bruce, who despite his own struggles, never lost hope in me or in my healing from the Lord. Also to my dear children, David and Esther, now both adults, who suffered themselves from my emotional brokenness, yet are now committed Christians receiving their own hope, healing and purpose from Jesus.

Contents

CHAPTER

CHAPTER 1

"Introduction"

Baby Joan was born on the third day of November 1930, during a time of World wide economic recession. Her mother rejected her, immediately after her birth, because she was born with a condition called "rickets." This affected the formation of the bones, and was often caused by malnutrition. Apparently, her mother had starved herself during the pregnancy, in order to have enough food to feed her other five children. Sadly she had been left a widow, as her husband had recently been killed at sea in mysterious circumstances.

Little Joan spent the first three years of her life in hospital, having one operation after another to try to improve the use of her legs, so she would be able to walk. During all this time, as far as is known, she received no visits at all from any family members. Time passed, and at three years of age, she was transferred from the hospital into the care of Dr Barnado's Homes, where she stayed until she was eight. Little is known about this period of Joan's life, but at the age of eight, she was "fostered" by a local couple. This couple practiced "spiritualism", and they also had living with them their elderly mother, who was also deeply involved in "spiritualism". This old lady had a powerful influence on Joan as she was growing up, and taught her many superstitious ideas and practices. The foster-parents believed that "god" had told them they would one day have a child of their own, if they would foster this semi-crippled girl.

The war years started when Joan was nine. She was allowed to go into the woods nearby and play with other children. There was a prisoner-of-war camp nearby, and Joan liked to go and visit, looking through the wire fence. Whilst other children would make fun of the prisoners, Joan wanted to talk to them.

Then quite suddenly, at the age of thirteen, Joan was rejected again, this time by her foster family. She was sent away from her home to Hampshire, to a special school for children suffering from physical or mental difficulties. Her foster parents had learnt that they were expecting a baby. Now that a child of their own was on the way, they felt they no longer had any need for Joan. She never saw nor heard from them again.

Two years later, as the war was ending, Joan made a momentous trip back to Devon to where her real mother and family were still living. She spent two or three weeks staying with them. It is not known how or why this visit happened or what took place during it, as there had been no contact between Joan and her family since her birth, but following her return to the school, a serious incident occurred. Joan became extremely ill, both emotionally and mentally, and she was transferred to a secure establishment for the mentally ill and criminally insane. She might have remained there for the rest of her life, but for an unexpected act nearly fifteen years later. An "unidentified" benefactor stepped in to rescue her from this establishment, securing her discharge by paying the sum of £100 for her release. This was a large sum of money in those days.

She was found a place to live in what was called a "Halfway House." She was able to work as a cleaner in a hospital for the elderly. It was now that a man over twenty years older saw her and took an interest in her. At first she tried to tell him to go away, but he became very persistent. The man's name was George. He had served time in the army, both in India and later in the Second World War, but was now suffering with alcoholism, symptoms relating to a head injury as a child and the traumas of war. Despite having been brought up on his parent's farm, and an army career, George now worked as a road sweeper for the local council.

Before long, Joan found that she was pregnant; she was now aged 30. She managed to get herself a job behind the bar in a local pub. Because she was on her feet a lot and growing larger with the pregnancy, her ankles became swollen; she was forced to rest in hospital six weeks prior to the birth of her baby. When the month of June arrived she gave birth to a baby girl, and that baby girl was **ME**.

CHAPTER 2

"A Baby Girl"

At the time of my birth, Mum and Dad were living in a little old caravan, on a site in a village in Hampshire. Dad would go out every night to the nearby village pub, and come back drunk, noisy and abusive.

Meanwhile, Mum, who had received no parental nurturing as an infant, did not know how to nurture me properly or even how to communicate with me. She struggled to meet a baby's basic needs. I was even given condensed milk in my bottle instead of powdered baby-milk! When I was about six months old, Dad, who had been drinking, picked up a kitchen knife and started to threaten Mum with it. In fear for her life, she took a swing at him with her fist and knocked him to the ground, unconscious. Then she ran for her life, away from the caravan, leaving me in my cot, alone with him. I stayed there unattended for two or maybe three days. By the end of that time, I must have been in a very neglected state, and it's a wonder I survived. Finally, Mum did return. She came when Dad was at work and took me away to the pub where she had previously worked as a barmaid. She had a room there where we could stay. It wasn't long before Dad began to turn up outside and make a nuisance of himself.

"Come back to me!" he would shout. "Come back to me!" The pub landlord often became very angry with him, and threatened him on more than one occasion. Finally, after a few months, Dad, in desperation, jumped off a railway bridge and broke one of his legs. It's hard to believe, but this persuaded Mum to go back to live with him. This time it was at his mother's house, located in a quiet street near the railway station.

Mum had become pregnant again, and was close to having the baby. In August of that year, when I was still only thirteen months old, the first of my brothers was born. They named him Johnny. At the time of his birth, I was taken away and placed with a temporary foster-family. I think they must have become quite attached to me, as they were reluctant to give me back. I was returned to Mum and Dad about three months later. Meanwhile, a new problem had arisen. Dad's Mother was insisting on taking care of Mum's new baby herself. Having had one boy and six girls of her own, she felt she knew best how to bring up a baby. She would not allow my Mum even to touch her baby boy. This greatly upset Mum, who felt that her baby had been snatched away from her. To make things worse, Dad's mother was very Victorian and severe in outlook and personality. She did not seem to like little girls, and she often threatened me when I was a toddler. She would wave her walking stick at me, shouting abuse and calling me nasty names. This continued for about eighteen months.

When I was a little over three years old, Mum gave birth to another baby, a girl, and they called her Sally. Soon after her birth, Mum and Dad moved from the house back to another caravan in a village outside town. Three small children and Mum and Dad, all living in her house, had become too much for the old lady to cope with. Not long after we had started living in this village, a traumatic set of events took place. Dad was still working by day as a road-sweeper, and drinking by night at the pub. Meanwhile Mum tried to look after three small children. One day she went to the village centre with us. She went into the local shop to buy something she needed, leaving Sally near the doorway in her pram, and Johnny outside in my care. (I was still only three years old, and Johnny was two).

Outside the shop there was a busy main road. To my horror, Johnny decided, just for the fun of it, to run across the main road. There was only one thing to do. I had to run across the road myself to fetch him back. Panting, and mercifully unharmed, I reached him. I tried to get him to run back to the shop with me, but he ran first and I had to follow. As I started to run, I noticed a big black car coming up the road. I didn't worry too much at first, since to me it seemed a long way off. Suddenly, the car was no longer far off. It was almost on top of us, and Johnny was running right into its path. The driver, a local schoolteacher, braked hard and swerved. The car missed Johnny, but in my anxiety I found myself running at full speed, straight into the front wing and bumper of the car. The impact sent me flying up into the air, and I landed on the car's windscreen. Then I rolled back down the windscreen and fell off the car onto the road. I remember lying in the road and being unable to move or get up. But I felt no pain, even though one of my legs was twisted in a strange position behind my back and neck. I could hear people shouting. Above them all, I could hear Mum's voice screaming at me,

"Your Dad will be so angry with you! He'll have to leave work early!"

All I could feel inside was a gnawing fear and dread, that I had done something very bad. I was already very frightened of Dad, so I didn't want him to come home, because I thought that if he came near me he would hurt me.

The ambulance arrived and I was carried inside, where they tried to make me comfortable. The driver turned the key in the ignition, but nothing happened. He tried again. Still the engine would not start. They had to take me out of the ambulance again. A Mini had stopped.

"Could I take her to the hospital?" said the driver.

"I'd be grateful if you would, mate," said the ambulance driver. "It would take too much time to call the station for another ambulance."

So I rode to the hospital in the Mini, accompanied by one of the ambulance men. I don't remember the journey, nor arriving at the hospital. I was given something to make me sleepy, and shortly afterwards I was taken for surgery. They found that both my legs were broken, with more than one break to my right leg. I also had two black eyes, but thankfully I received no serious head or internal injuries. I believe that even in these early years that God was watching over me and had spared my life.

There now followed a period of several months in a hospital bed with my legs in traction, mostly in a room all by myself. There was a rocking horse at the bottom of my bed. I was a bit frightened of it at first, as I didn't know what it was. The room had a glass partition beyond the rocking horse, and I could see prams lined up on the other side. Sometimes I could see a nurse put a baby or toddler in a pram and take them off somewhere. I so much wanted someone to come and take me out, as I felt trapped by not being able to move, but nobody came. I wanted to see Mum, but she didn't come to visit me. In fact, nobody from my family came to visit. I felt abandoned, afraid that I would be there forever and never see any of them again. Because I had given up hope, I became very quiet and withdrawn. This may also have been the reason I wet the bed every night. It made the nurses cross with me, which did not help. They would mutter and moan as they were forced to move my "equipment" and me to another bed. In the end, they gave up and put me in nappies! I also upset the staff by refusing to eat (I did eat ice cream and jelly), and sometimes I would throw the food on the floor in my frustration.

During all this time, I have no memory of anyone who was really kind to me or even talked to me. I never cried; Dad did not like any noise or crying, and I had become too frightened to cry for fear of being hurt. Eventually, I went back to the caravan with my legs in plaster, though I don't remember how I got there. I don't recall any greetings or emotions from the family on my return home, and I became more and more emotionally distant, especially towards Mum. I remember playing outside with Johnny and splashing in the puddles with my "plaster" legs.

Mum was expecting a baby yet again, and we were moved back into the nearby town. This time it was to a two bedroom council house in a very run-down area, with a river nearby. At night, what seemed like hundreds of cockroaches would come into the kitchen and the downstairs of the house. There was an outside toilet, which was cold and damp; and the house was always dirty, as Mum could no longer cope with housework. We only had a tin bath for washing and bathing, and no hot water. The only heating in the house was one open fire in the living room.

The time came for Mum to have her next child and she went off to hospital. That evening a car pulled up and a man and a woman got out. I didn't know who they were, and couldn't think what they wanted with us. They came into the house and picked up Sally, who was about 19 months old at the time. Then they carried her out to the car, climbed in, and drove off. I could see her red face as the car pulled away, and I could hear her screaming. Dazed and bewildered, I wondered if I would ever see her again. Dad was shouting and swearing at them because Sally was his favourite, his pet. But they took her away all the same. Next morning, early, the same two people came back and put Johnny and me into their car. This time there was no reaction from Dad. They took us to a house in the town, where there was a woman with two children of similar age to us. The first thing the woman said to us was,

"You children are not allowed to touch or play with any of my children's toys."

Johnny did not really understand and ran out into the garden and jumped on their tricycle. The woman started shouting angrily at him to get off the tricycle. He did get off, but then started to throw stones, which made her become even angrier with him. Meanwhile I stayed very quiet and would not speak a word. I wanted to run and hide. Later that day the woman became aggressive towards Johnny and began to hit him. This was because she was trying to get him ready for bed and he was being difficult with her. I was so fearful of her that somehow I managed to go through that night without wetting the bed, something that I had been doing every night before then.

The next day, the same people came again with their car, and took Johnny and me back home to Dad. He fed us on Weetabix and Corn flakes, and went to work leaving us on our own each day. We would spend our time playing Cowboys and Indians round the nearby garages and helping ourselves to apples on display at the front of the corner shop. I have no memory of any adults being around, except that there was sometimes an old man in one of the garages where we used to play. I remember that he used to give me sweets and he would play music on an old wind-up gramophone. He seemed kind and talked to us and took an interest in us. I liked this at first, as I was not used to kind treatment and being talked to. However I also remember that the old man would lift me up and touch me in places that would make me feel bad inside. My brother, Johnny, would want to go back to see the old man because there were all sorts of interesting things in the garage for him to play with. I didn't like going there because of the things the old man tried to do, and because he insisted that his wife must not know we were in his garage.

After his work was finished for the day, Dad would come home and give us Weetabix or Corn flakes again. Then he would take us with him to the pub around the corner. We would have to wait out on the roadside for a few hours in all weathers whilst he was inside, drinking. Sometimes he would bring us out a packet of crisps and a bottle of coke. Eventually he would come out of the pub, having had a lot to drink, and we would follow him home. He would be agitated, bad-tempered and jumpy.

"We're under attack!" he would shout. "It's the Indians! They're hiding behind those bushes."

Sometimes it would be Indians, and sometimes Germans, waiting for him under his bed. I was completely bewildered. I had no idea what Germans were, and I thought Indians were men with feathers on their heads, who fought with Cowboys! Once Johnny and I were in our beds, we were so tired that we slept through the night. We were never washed, and had no changes of clothes during the time that Mum was away. As a result, I started to develop boils on my legs and arms. They were painful, especially when I knocked them on anything.

When the weekend came, Dad would take us to visit the local slaughterhouse. He seemed to know the people who worked there. He would take us round the inside of the building where cows and pigs were being slaughtered. I hated it, because I knew that the animals were being killed. The pigs would let out loud squeals of fear, which caused me great distress, because I liked animals. I would watch the cows walking in line, and then suddenly there would be a loud bang, the floor would open, and the cow would fall through. I just wanted to leave the place and go home. We went repeatedly over a period of about three years. On later trips Dad would take my brothers and sister too, but Mum never went. I hated it every time, but I couldn't get out of it.

After two weeks or so, Mum returned from the hospital with my second brother. They named him Richard. It was a few more weeks before Sally also returned. The more children there were in the household, the more difficult it became for Mum and Dad to cope. The atmosphere in the home became increasingly dark.

CHAPTER 3

"Starting school"

Just one month later, I experienced another upheaval. I was very nearly five years old, and was due to start school. I remember walking to the school with Mum. It was about ten minutes from our house. She had told me nothing about why we were going there, and said nothing during the walk. I had no idea what to expect. When we arrived, Mum left me without saying good-bye. In my five year-old mind, I thought I had been left in a big home for children. I spent all morning in great anxiety, but without speaking a word. Eventually at lunchtime, I plucked up all my courage and asked the teacher,

"Where are the beds?" She looked taken aback. "Beds?" she echoed.

She explained reassuringly that this was a school, and that I would be going home again later that afternoon. This was a big relief to me. Although I was quite with-drawn, I somehow learnt quickly to read and write. I especially loved listening to the teacher reading us stories; I liked playing with the sand and water and I enjoyed learning songs and singing. I remember making a friend called Jenny. I also remember making a little egg-cosy, which I took home for Mum, but she didn't seem interested in it.

Meanwhile the atmosphere at home was going from bad to worse. Dad became very abusive towards my brother Johnny, and sometimes towards me. One of his habits involved him standing near the front door and calling for us in a loud and aggressive voice. As we obeyed the call to "Get in!" we would have to come past him into the house. As we did so, Dad would hit us round the head hard. It hurt a lot, and knocked us off balance. One time I did fall over, hit my head, and developed a bump the size of an egg on my forehead. Not surprisingly, I was becoming even more nervous and afraid of Dad. I started to stay indoors to avoid trouble. There was a wooden table in the kitchen with a green-check tablecloth on it, which hung down near the floor. On this table there was a teapot; Dad's cup and saucer; Mum's cup and saucer; a milk jug; a bowl of sugar and two plates, one each for Mum and Dad. This became my special hiding place, where I felt safe, and I would have my one-and-only Cindy doll under the table with me. I would stay there for hours, from the time that Dad came home from work until he left for the pub. During these times, he would swear, shout and swipe at anyone who got in his way or under his feet. We had no television, but just a portable battery powered radio, which always played BBC Radio Two non-stop from morning till night.

One Sunday evening Dad came home after drinking heavily at the pub. He was in an angry and aggressive mood, and started shouting at the top of his voice, swearing, and banging his fist on the kitchen table, with me hiding underneath. This he had done many times before, and it always made me jump out of my skin; the shock would go through my body. This time, he was especially violent and the force of his fist broke the table in two. I had no way to escape. A piece of the table landed on me and stuck into my chest. I was shocked and in pain, and was nearly knocked out, because the table had also hit my head. When I went to school next day, the school nurse asked me lots of questions about the big bump on my head. A few days later we had a visit from two social workers. Dad was very rude and insulting to them. He lied and told them that I had tripped over the carpet and banged my head on the wall. Nothing more was said or done at the time.

One day when I was at school, the old man with the garage round the corner came and knocked on our door with a bag of groceries. Mum accepted the groceries eagerly, and the old man took the opportunity of offering to help her with bathing the kids in the evening when Dad was in the pub. Once again the old man did things to me, but as far as I know he did not touch any of the others. I remember that he didn't want Mum or the rest of us to tell his wife that he had been round to our house. Even so, these visits continued for about three years, until we moved house. He was always giving food and money to Mum, and sweets to us.

Johnny started school the following April. He would never stay for long and kept on running away. It seemed to us that almost all the other children called us rude names, shouting that we were full of fleas. We also used to have stones thrown at us on the way to and from school. I found this taunting very upsetting, and I worried about my brother. I became more and more timid and withdrawn and wanted the ground to swallow me up, but little Johnny became more and more angry, and would shout and throw stones back at the bullies. Sadly, a day came when Johnny struck an older ringleader with a metal object. That same day Johnny was taken away, and I did not see him again for several months.

One August morning a short time later, I came downstairs early to find Mum, who had been looking fat again, sitting on a chair in the kitchen, moaning in pain.

"Mum!" I said. "What's the matter?"

She said, "Your Father's gone off to work and left me like this. I'm having the baby! Get an ambulance, quickly!"

I ran out the house thinking, "I've got to go to the hospital to get an ambulance," but at six years old I couldn't remember how to get there. All I knew was that it was at the top of the town. I ran as fast as I could for about half a mile. When I reached the High Street, a kind man and woman stopped me.

"What's the hurry, little girl?" they asked. "Is something wrong?"

I replied, "Mum is having a baby! I need to find the hospital to get an ambulance for her. Can you tell me where it is?" "You don't need to go to the hospital to get an ambulance," they said. "Do you know where your house is? Is your Mum there now?"

"Yes, she is," I said.

"Well, you go on back home," they replied, "and we'll call an ambulance for your Mum."

By the time I reached home, Mum had already left. She gave birth to another baby boy in the ambulance on the way to the hospital. They named my third brother, Jeffrey. Whilst Mum was away in hospital, Dad continued to go both to work in the daytime and to the pub at night. Johnny was still away, and I was left to look after my sister Sally (3) and baby Richard (16 months), as well as myself. I managed to block up the toilet with Richard's terry nappies, and got into big trouble from Dad. Meanwhile we were back to eating cereals every morning and evening.

Mum was away for about two weeks, and during that stay they insisted that she should have an operation to stop her having any more babies. When she came home, she could not cope at all with the new baby. During the night, the baby was screaming, and Dad shouted for me to go downstairs to get a bottle out of the fridge to feed the baby. I had to find my way downstairs in the dark, past the cockroaches, to get to the fridge to fetch the bottle. I did not know that the milk should be warmed, so I came back upstairs and put a bottle of cold milk into the baby's mouth.

I had to take him, with his carrycot, into the bedroom I already shared with Sally and Richard, and the next morning I was told to bring him downstairs. I picked him up, and had reached the top of the stairs, when suddenly he wriggled in my arms. This gave me such a fright that I let go of him, and he bounced right down the stairs from the top to the bottom. I felt terrible, thinking I had killed my baby brother. I had to run down the stairs and pick him up again, and to my relief he started to wail. Over the next six weeks, I had to feed him, change his nappies and his clothes, and I would spend a lot of time taking him outside in a pram. To me he was like a baby doll, to play with. Then, at six weeks old, Jeffrey became very ill. We didn't realise until, unexpectedly, Dad decided one evening to take Jeffrey with him to the pub, in order to show him off to his drinking buddies. Dad had never done this with the rest of us. One of the men in the pub became alarmed by how the baby looked. He said,

"George, your baby looks half-dead to me. I think he needs to go to the hospital straight away."

Amazingly, Dad agreed to go with this man, who took Jeffrey in his car to the hospital. Sure enough, Jeffrey was found to be very ill with double pneumonia and collapsed lungs. He was immediately admitted and placed in an incubator. Jeffrey stayed in the hospital for several weeks. Once again, I believe that God stepped in to save a life in our family.

While Jeffrey was away, Johnny returned to us. I still do not know where he had been taken. He liked to mix with older boys in the local area, and was lured by them into petty crime. Dad started to get increasingly angry and violent towards Johnny, and would hit him. One day Johnny had done something wrong, and he could not escape from the house. I was coming downstairs when suddenly Johnny came tearing up the stairs with Dad chasing him, brandishing a garden rake with a long wooden handle and metal prongs. I turned and fled back upstairs. I ran into Mum and Dad's room and hid under their low double bed, getting as far under as I could to be next to the wall. Johnny dived after me and pushed in next to me. Meanwhile Dad, who was very angry, was trying to pull us out from under the bed by using the rake. Both Johnny and I were shaking like leaves with fear. The rake did not touch me, but I believe that Johnny was scratched by it on his back. After a long time, Dad gave up and went out to the pub, and Johnny and I were able to come downstairs. Johnny went out, and I hid under the replacement kitchen table. Strangely, nothing was ever said about this incident.

After a few weeks, Jeffrey came back from hospital. Once again, I was given responsibility to feed and change him. Mum was spending a lot of time now just sitting by the radio, rocking backwards and forwards on a wooden chair, and complaining of having hot flushes. Meanwhile, I had to play more and more of the mother's role in the family. Much of the time I would have to look after the three youngest children, whilst Johnny would be out playing round by the garages with the older local boys.

Chapter 4

"Moving house again"

I was seven years old when the Council moved us to a three-bedroom house in another part of the town. It was about a twenty-minute walk from our old house, and was three storeys high, with two bedrooms on the top storey. Johnny and Richard shared one bedroom and Sally and I shared the other with baby Jeffrey. On the next floor down was a bedroom for Mum and Dad, and a spare room that was used as a storage-room. (Later, men from the Council came and converted it into a bathroom). A staircase led down to the basement, in which was a sitting room, a kitchen with a cooker and a big sink. At the back was a lean-to porch, with a toilet in it. There was no central heating, but there was a coal fire in the sitting room. Our bedrooms at the top of the house became very cold in winter, and ice formed even on the inside of the windows. The house felt very cold and dark, and it was always dirty inside.

Johnny and I had to change to a new school, which was just across the road. Sally started school for the first time. It was a relief to have left behind the old school and the kids who bullied us and called us names.

Johnny quickly made friends with some older boys. I made friends with two girls, who were sisters, the older one being in my class. One afternoon, only a few days after starting school, Sally was in the sitting room, playing near the open fire. Dad was sitting in the armchair near the fireplace, which was always his favourite spot. By accident, one of my brothers pushed Sally backwards. She tripped over the hearth, lost her balance, and fell back into the fire, letting out a loud scream. Dad reacted very quickly. He reached down and pulled Sally off the grate and out of the fire with his bare hands. Sally was still yelling and screaming in pain. Mum came hurrying over and together they rubbed margarine over the burns. This only made her scream even more. An hour or so later she was still screaming, so they told me to get an ambulance.

This time I knew what to do; I went down the road to the telephone box and dialled 999. Soon an ambulance came to the house and took Sally to the hospital, where she stayed overnight. She returned the next day, while I was at school.

After school the next day, I was looking after my brothers and sister again. I was pushing an old wooden cart up and down the road with Richard and Jeffrey sitting on it. Sally was also on it, but she was lying face down on her front, as she couldn't sit down; she was moaning and crying all the time. Someone had removed the protective bandaging and covering that had been placed over the burns, which were right across the upper back of both her legs. As we passed a house, which was further up our road, a lady was just opening her front door. Hearing all the noise, she hurried out to ask me what was wrong. I explained to her what had happened to Sally. Then she said,

"I am a nurse. May I please take a look at her burns?"

I agreed, so she took a look. Then she asked me,

"What are your names?"

When I told her, she replied,

"Do you come from George's house down the road?"

Then she said, "My name is Julie Beck. I used to work at the hospital. Sally should not have been released so soon, and your parents should not have left you to look after her. She must go back to the hospital immediately and have proper treatment and care. I am going to call an ambulance for her."

Very soon the ambulance came to take Sally back to the hospital. This time she was gone for about a week.

Meanwhile, Johnny was having more and more problems, both at school and at home. At school, the head-teacher was always hitting Johnny. This upset me a lot, because Dad was also hitting Johnny at home. On more than one occasion, Johnny escaped through the sitting room window, smashing through the pane of glass as he did so, just to get away from Dad. Johnny began to spend even more time away from both home and school. Often he would go into town with older boys and get into petty crime. Several times Johnny was brought back to the school or to our house in a police car; and he was still only six years old.

All this time, Mum was becoming more mentally ill. She would talk at me a great deal, and also she would make "monkey" faces at us through the window. Then she would sometimes dance the "Can-Can" in the kitchen, thinking that she was performing in a show. She would even try to boil a kettle on the stove, without putting any water in it. She was constantly making herself cups of tea and smoking cigarettes almost non-stop. The only practical things that she was able to do were the washing and the washing up.

On one occasion, completely out of the blue, we had a visit from Dad's mother, accompanied by one of Dad's sisters. They came into our house, and sat themselves down on wooden chairs in the sitting room. Dad was out at work, so they started to talk to Mum. Meanwhile, Johnny and I were playing "Cowboys and Indians" in the sitting room. As part of the game, we started rolling about on the floor together, near to where the old lady was sitting. Suddenly and without warning, she started hitting me across my back with her walking stick. She also swore at me, calling me nasty names, and telling me to leave Johnny alone. At that very moment, little Jeffrey, who was sitting in his highchair on the other side of the room, picked up his teaspoon and threw it at her. Amazingly the spoon hit the old lady on the top of her head. She stopped hitting me, and turned her angry gaze on the toddler. She began to get off her chair with her stick raised in the air, shouting and threatening Jeffrey. I realised that she was going to hit him with her stick. I managed to run over, lift him out of his chair, and carry him outside into the street. I then hid with him in an alleyway for a long time, until she had left. That was the last time I ever saw Dad's mother.

One day, I became very upset about the things that the head teacher was doing to Johnny, and I blurted it out to Mum. Normally she didn't react to this sort of thing.

On this occasion however, she went over to the school, still in her nightdress, barged into the head teachers' room, and picked up a wooden chair. She then waved it in the air, shouting at him to stop bullying her son Johnny, because he was already getting enough of that from his Dad. When I got to school a few minutes later, the kids were laughing at me and taunting me, saying that my Mum was a crazy nutcase. I just wanted to disappear into the ground. In the future though, the head teacher avoided Mum whenever he saw her nearby.

A few days later, I came back from school to find Mum in a stressed-out state. She told me that Johnny was at the police station with Dad. There had been a fire in a petrol tanker, and the police thought that Johnny was involved. He was allowed to come home that evening, but Johnny and I, with Dad, had to go down to the Police Station after school every day that week. The police took me into a room with Dad, and asked me lots of questions about Johnny. They wanted to know where we went together and what we did. I was too scared to tell them about the things Dad did to him, because Dad was with me in the room. I was frightened because I thought I might be in trouble too. Within a few weeks, Johnny had to go to Court, and Mum and Dad went with him. When I got back from school that afternoon, Mum was muttering,

"Johnny is going to be taken away for a long time, but it's for his own good."

The next day was a Saturday. Dad was down at the pub in the afternoon when a car with a policeman and a policewoman arrived outside the house. Mum was scared and was hiding in the kitchen, so I had to answer the door to them. The policewoman said to me,

"We have come to take Johnny for an outing. Where is he?" At that moment, he was hiding behind Dad's chair in the sitting room.

"He doesn't want to go on an outing with you!" I said.

"If he gets in the car with us, he can have all these sweets," she replied, producing two bags of sweets and showing them to me.

"Johnny doesn't want your sweets. Go away!" I retorted.

"Oh, don't be like that;" she replied gently. "We only want to take Johnny on an outing. We'll bring him back by tonight. He can have lots and lots of ice cream, and whatever he wants, if he will just get in the car with us."

"No you're not," I replied, "you want to take him away for good."

But the temptation of sweets and ice cream was too much for Johnny. I tried to stop him going by telling him that he wouldn't be coming back, but he came out of hiding, got into the Police car and they left. I felt very sad because I didn't think I would ever see Johnny again.

CHAPTER 5

"Fear and Trauma"

One evening, when I was eight years old and Johnny was still away, I was told by Dad to go and get some fish and chips. The nearest chip shop was quite a long way from our house. I was also told to take Sally, Richard and Jeffrey with me. I had already taken them out to the park earlier in the day, using our big "Silver Cross" pram for Jeffrey and Richard. I used to push this pram every day during school holidays and weekends, because Mum wanted us all out of the house. On this occasion, I had Jeffrey at the top of the pram and Richard at the bottom. Dad had given me a ten-shilling note to pay for the food, and I was told not to lose it and to bring back the change. I decided to put the note under the pram mattress and I had Richard sitting on top.

I was feeling tired, as I had been out with them all for most of the day. I was also in a hurry, so I decided to take a short cut, following a pathway that lead uphill and then down again. The downhill slope was much steeper than I had expected. The pram felt very heavy, and to my dismay it started to run away. I had to run with it, but I would not let go.

I shouted to Sally,

"Put the brake on! Put the brake on Sally!"

She tried to, but she could not run fast enough to keep up. Then I started to panic. There was a metal fence coming up in front of us, the path turned sharply, and then another short steep hill led straight down to a busy main road.

Richard and Jeffrey had realised that something was wrong, and they were both screaming loudly. As I reached the sharp turn and the metal fence, I somehow managed to tip the pram over onto its side, whilst still running at full speed. There was a horrible noise as the pram scraped along the ground and came to a standstill against the metal fence. I was dragged along the ground, still holding onto the pram, and I scraped the skin off both of my arms and legs. Sally was still following further behind, so she escaped without any injury. Richard had fallen out of the pram when it tipped over; he was screaming. He had injured his arm, and three of his fingers looked broken. Jeffrey was still inside the pram, but he had somehow hit his head, and it was now bleeding badly. I knew that I had to get help, so I picked myself up from the pathway and went running down the last hill. Halfway down this hill there was a garden gate. Two ladies and a man, having heard all the noise and screaming, were coming out of it.

"Whatever is going on?" one of them asked me, as I ran up to them.

"The pram tipped over and my brother's head is bleeding badly," I panted, all out of breath.

One of the people went back inside their house to call for help, while the other two hurried up to where the pram was, still lying on the ground. They carried Richard and Jeffrey back to their house to see to their injuries and to wait for help to arrive. Meanwhile, I was desperately searching all round the pram, inside and outside. I had remembered the ten-shilling note that Dad had given me, but I couldn't find it anywhere. The lady came back and asked why I was so stressed out about the note.

"Dad told me not to lose it," I said, "and I'm really scared that he'll hurt me if I don't have it."

She went into her house and quickly came out with another ten-shilling note.

"There you are," she said, giving it to me. "Pretend that you never lost it."

Very soon, the Police arrived and Dad was with them. The first thing Dad asked me was,

"Have you got my ten bob note? Give it here then."

I gave him the one I had been given by the kind lady. The Police took Richard and Jeffrey to the hospital and Dad went with them in the Police car. Meanwhile, I had to walk back home with Sally. I was still in pain from my cuts and bruises. We had to leave the pram where it was because it was too broken to push anymore. Jeffrey stayed in hospital over night and had some stitches in his head, but Richard came home with Dad, with his fingers strapped and his arm in a sling.

A few weeks after all this, a man came to visit Dad. He was in his early thirties, and he arrived dressed in an army uniform. I had seen him once before when I was younger, at our old house, when he had come to visit us with a lady and two children. This time he was on his own. It turned out that he was coming to stay for a while.

This man was the son of my Dad's sister, so he was really my cousin, but we were told to call him Uncle Bill. Dad gave him Richard's room as Johnny was still away, and Richard had to come in with Sally and me. Jeffrey had to sleep in my bed with me.

At first it was quite fun having Uncle Bill in the house, and he would sometimes play games with us. But then he started grabbing hold of me, and touching me in ways I didn't like. Gradually he began to be more rough and aggressive towards me. Sometimes he would trap me in the corner of a room, and put his hands around my neck. At that point, his eyes would turn red. Then in the middle of the night, when it was just starting to get light, he would come into my room and force Jeffrey out of my bed and into Sally's bed. He would get into my bed and put his hand over my mouth, telling me to be quiet, while molesting me and forcing me to do things to him. He would say, "When you're sixteen, I'm coming to get you, and then you'll be mine, all mine." I was very frightened and didn't ever want to be sixteen. He also threatened my life outside the house. He took me to the weirs, where the river flows fast into a mill, and dangled me over the water by my feet. He threatened to let go and drop me if I said anything to anybody, and if I didn't do what he wanted. Sometimes I managed to run away from him but I never told anybody what was going on. I just wanted him to go away from our house and to leave me alone. I never wanted to see him again.

Early one Sunday evening, Uncle Bill asked Mum if he could take Jeffrey and me to the evening service at the Salvation Army chapel, in the centre of town. This was very unexpected. Mum said that Jeffrey was too young, which was unlike her, but that he could take Richard instead. We walked into town with Uncle Bill holding our hands, and arrived at the chapel. We all went in but, three or four minutes later while they were singing the first hymn, Uncle Bill looked at us and said,

"This is too boring. Come on, let's go to the park!"

He took Richard and me by the hand, and took us straight past the swings and the play area. He kept walking all the way to the wild marshland at the very far end of the park, beyond the playing fields. He kept telling us that we were all going to see the pheasants. Richard and I pleaded with him to let us go back to play on the swings, but he said that we would do that later. We reached the marshland by the river, and Uncle Bill suddenly pushed me violently onto my back on the ground. Then he grabbed hold of Richard by the back of his coat, lifted him off the ground, and held him over the flowing river.

"Be quiet, both of you!" he said. "If either of you makes any noise or shouts or screams, I will kick Richard into the river like a football."

His voice was cold and callous. He put Richard down on the riverbank, and turned to me. I had been trying to get up, but I was shocked by being knocked to the ground and by seeing Richard dangling over the water. Uncle Bill grabbed me, and took off my underwear, which he put in his pocket. Then he got on top of me on the wet ground and raped me. I felt like I was having my insides ripped out and that it would never end. I also felt as if my whole head was going to explode. I wanted to scream, but I could not. After it was over, he made me stand up, but my legs felt like jelly. I felt dazed and shaken, almost as if it had all been a bad dream. I remember asking Uncle Bill to give me back my underwear, but he ignored me and would not do so. Meanwhile, Richard had been sitting very still and quiet on the riverbank, having seen what had happened. Uncle Bill took hold of our hands again, very tightly, and walked back towards the town. It was nearly dark by now and we reached a little corner-shop near the edge of the park. Uncle Bill told us that we could have all the sweets we wanted, but if we told anyone that we had been to the park instead of the chapel, or what he had done, he would kill us. This put great fear into me. In the shop, Richard chose lots of sweets, but I didn't want any at all from Uncle Bill. Instead, I wanted to run round the corner to the Police station to tell them what had happened. But I couldn't do this because he had hold of my hand so tightly.

Next morning when I went to the toilet I found that I was bleeding down my legs. I was so scared that I thought I was going to die. I told Mum, and she saw the blood for herself. She took me to the doctor's surgery without making an appointment, but before we left home, Uncle Bill threatened again to kill me if I said anything about what he had done to me. We went in to see the doctor, and Mum said to him that Uncle Bill had interfered with her daughter. The doctor asked me no questions and did not even examine me. Instead he gave Mum a funny look and told her to "tell me about the birds and the bees." On arriving home, I was cornered again by Uncle Bill.

"What did you tell the doctor?" he demanded.

"Nothing," I replied. "The doctor didn't even look at me." Meanwhile, Mum was moaning about the way the doctor had treated us.

A few days later, my school friend came to our house to play. Somehow, Uncle Bill managed to get alone with her; a few minutes later she went running out of our house in a very frightened state. After a few more days, a rumour started going round the local pub that this girl's dad was coming to get Uncle Bill, and he was planning to shoot him with his rabbit gun. Uncle Bill got to hear of this rumour and suddenly left our house. I never saw him again. I heard later that he had been sent to prison and had been given a life sentence.

CHAPTER 6

"Forth House"

Six months passed, during which time we had a visit from two ladies, who brought food for Mum, and clothing and shoes for us. I didn't know who they were. Apparently they were from a charity trying to help poor families. They talked to us about a house in the country; they said that our family would be going there for a holiday quite soon. I didn't know what to make of it all, as I was suspicious of them. I didn't really want to leave my home or my friends.

A month or so later, one morning in early spring, a minibus pulled up outside our house. One of the ladies, who had visited us before, got out and knocked at the door. When we answered the door, she asked Sally, Richard, Jeffrey and myself to get into the minibus, and then Mum. We did so, thinking that we were going on a holiday break for Mum. Then she tried to get Dad into the minibus. He stubbornly refused. She spent nearly half an hour trying, and there was a lot of shouting.

"You really must come!" she was telling him. "You can't leave your wife and children."

He replied, "I am not coming. I have my job to go to and my house. If I go with you, they will take away my house and I will lose my job."

Finally, he turned back into the house, slammed the door in her face, and locked it. She gave up and left him behind. I was pleased he didn't come. It seemed a long journey. At long last, the minibus turned into a very long driveway leading up to Forth House. I was amazed at the size of the house. I had never seen such a big house before. The front of the house had a big door leading into a porch. I noticed that all the glass windows in the porch had been broken, and this worried me. The minibus driver said she would take us on a tour around the house. As we entered the large front door, we saw a big staircase to the right with banisters on either side. To the left was a door into a very large sitting room, which had settees, armchairs, and a TV. in the corner. This was the first time that I had seen a TV. I felt excited at the thought of watching it. Past the staircase and to the right, there was also a big dining room, with a number of tables, together with chairs round them. There was also a big kitchen, but no children were allowed in it. The minibus driver then took us up the staircase to show us where our rooms were. As we entered, we saw a bedroom with a window and a double bed. There was a door to the left, which led through to another bedroom with two double bunk beds. This room also had a window. From the main bedroom there was another door leading to a little room with a W.C. and sink. There was no kitchen or living room. This, then, must be our family accommodation. There was a communal bathroom upstairs, and the communal sitting room and dining room downstairs. Also downstairs, in a separate building at the back, there was a washhouse for the mothers to do their laundry.

The grounds of the house were massive, with trees, a little river, a large lawn and some toys to play with. I felt excited about the grounds because I loved the freedom of being outside and able to do what I wanted. For the first week, we were allowed to play outside in the grounds and watch TV. in the sitting room. It felt like a holiday for us and Mum seemed to be better, because she didn't have to cook or clean. Also, things were much better for us without Dad around. Soon, however, I began to find the atmosphere in the big house creepy and scary, and I began to sleep in the big bed with Mum. There were several other families living in the house, and they all seemed to be poor and to have different problems. At night, some of the men would come back to the house from the local pub, drunk. There would often be shouting, fighting and arguing, and even the sound of glass bottles breaking. Sometimes I could hear women or children shouting and screaming from their bedrooms, and I found it all very frightening. Mum also was becoming very nervous, especially as we had no key for our room, and we could not lock our door. She became scared. She had heard from one of the other women that there was a particular man staying there who was known to have a violent temper. Word was that he also carried a knife. Mum started to moan and complain that she hated the place and she wanted to go home. She had made one or two friends, who were similar to herself. I didn't really make any friends, but spent my time mostly in the grounds with my sister and brothers.

After the first week had passed, on Monday morning we were told that we were going to the local school with some of the other children living in the house. At first, we didn't have school uniforms, but we got these later. Richard was due to start at a pre-school for the first time, as he had just turned four. But when it was time to go, he threw himself on the ground, kicking and screaming and refusing to go. He had to be carried onto the minibus still making a loud hullabaloo. Sally and I got on the same minibus for the school, quietly and without making any fuss. However, I felt scared inside and did not want to go. I did not want to be part of this school; I decided I would shut myself off and not talk to anyone. I acted this way for the whole term, and I ended up feeling very lonely and isolated. I was completely left out. A few children tried to be friendly to me at the start, but they soon gave up when I continued to give them the cold shoulder. Because I was so lonely, I escaped and walked back to Forth House on more than one occasion, but each time, I was taken straight back to school again.

We had been at Forth House for about a month, when we had a visit from Dad. He stayed for the weekend. I can remember coming back from school to find him there, and I felt anxiety about it. Mum seemed pleased to see him, but I was forced to move back to a bunk bed in the other bedroom. Each Saturday, all the children had to go in the minibus to "Saturday Morning Cinema." This was at the nearby local cinema and I enjoyed it. When we got back from the cinema this particular Saturday, we found Mum all by herself. Dad had gone off to the local pub with some of the other men, and he stayed there until closing time. On the Sunday, after breakfast,

Dad left in the minibus to go home again, so we saw very little of him that weekend. Over the next few weeks, Dad made one or two more weekend visits. They all followed a similar pattern. He would usually be rude and un-cooperative towards the staff of the house because he did not want to be forced to stay.

About six weeks after our arrival at Forth House, a new family arrived. It consisted of a husband, a wife; a daughter aged four and a baby. One morning, I was in the dining room by myself, getting my cereal from the table, when the man came up behind me and picked me up in his arms. Then he turned me towards him and rubbed me up and down against his body.

"Let go of me!" I said. "Put me down! Stop it!"

I felt scared, anxious and fearful that he was going to hurt me. At that moment, somebody came into the dining room; to my relief, he quickly let me go. To my horror, that day and every weekday, he got on the school minibus as he had some job locally. Every time I saw him I would try to stay as far away from him as possible. There were other times when he would try to grab hold of me, but I always managed to avoid him. I felt angry inside, so to get back at him, and with Sally's help, we lifted his little daughter up between us and twice threw her into a bed of stinging nettles, which were growing in the grounds. Nothing was ever said about it, but after-wards I would feel bad about what I had done. I felt sorry for the child, as it wasn't her fault.

At half term, we had a very unexpected visit. It was from my brother, Johnny. I was pleased and relieved to see him again. I quickly showed him all the good places to play around the grounds. We played our old games together, like "Cowboys and Indians", and Sally, Richard and Jeffrey all tried to join in. Other children also tried to join our games, but Johnny clashed with another boy of about his age. They had a fight and the other boy finished up in the river. Because of this, Johnny had to leave and go back again to wherever he had come from. His visit had lasted only three or four days. I was sad that he had to leave.

The local school closed for the summer holidays, so we spent all day long at Forth House. Each week they would take the parents and children on a days' outing. At the start of the third week of the holidays, Dad arrived to spend a whole week with us. Again he spent a lot of time at the pub, and he seemed to enjoy the company of one or two of the other men. One weekday Dad, Mum and all of us went on an outing, together with the other families. They took us all in three minibuses to a pond where people could paddle or swim. There was an area where parents could sit in deck chairs. There was also a green nearby, and across the green there were a few shops and a pub. Dad and his friend went to buy ice creams for everyone with money given to him by the staff. While Dad was doing this, I waded into the pond and suddenly stepped on something very sharp under the water. I started to make my way back to Mum who was sitting on a deck chair, but as soon as I came out of the water, the man who had previously grabbed me at Forth House, grabbed me again. Lifting me up in his arms, he started calling for help. I hated being in his arms, and I was in a state of shock. Then I realised that I was bleeding heavily from my foot. Two or three women came running across with some towels. They pressed them tightly against my foot. Nearby there was a first aid shelter. For some reason there was a long queue of people waiting to see the first-aid person. But the man who was carrying me pushed right past the whole queue, and took me straight in. They took one look at my toe.

"That needs to be stitched," they said. "This child needs to go to the hospital immediately."

One of the minibus drivers said that she would take me straight away. To my relief, the man carrying me was told to put me down on a seat in the minibus, while one of the ladies stayed with me, holding the towel around my foot. By this time, Dad had arrived back with the ice creams. The lady in charge told Dad to hand over the ice creams and go with me in the minibus. He obeyed. Neither Dad nor I got an ice cream that day!

This whole incident was very frightening to me. I was terrified at the thought of having stitches in my foot, and I didn't really want to have Dad with me. When I arrived at the hospital, I was taken straight into a room, where a man in a white coat gave me some tablets to make me drowsy and an injection to numb my foot. My big toe was almost severed; they had to spend quite a long time sewing it back on again. I had to lie on a bed with my foot up on a support. Meanwhile Dad sat on a chair and the doctor was describing what he was doing. When they had finished, my foot was bandaged up and Dad and I were taken back to Forth House in the minibus. My foot stayed bandaged for at least ten days, and I had to go back to see a nurse on more than one occasion to have the dressing changed and the stitches checked. This meant that I was not able to run around or play very much in the grounds. I stayed inside watching television. At the end of the week, Dad went back home. After he had gone, Mum started getting agitated and homesick. By now she had been placed on the job rota for the women, which included cleaning the house, kitchen duties, and occasionally helping to supervise the Saturday morning cinema trips. She found these duties too much for her to cope with. One Saturday morning, it was her first time to do the cinema duty. We were all waiting in the minibus, ready to go, and I was quite excited to have Mum coming with us, as she had never been before. We were waiting and waiting; some staff members and parents were looking for Mum, but she could not be found anywhere. Eventually, another mother took her place, and we went off without her. I was very disappointed and worried. I couldn't enjoy the trip that day, as I was anxious about Mum. When we got back to Forth House, there was still no sign of her. Nobody knew where she was. That night, one of the staff came and slept on top of Mum's bed with her clothes on, and I slept in the same bed as usual. I couldn't really sleep because I was filled with fear and anxiety, thinking that Mum had abandoned us and would never return. This went on for another day and another night. I kept asking if they had found Mum and when she would be coming back. They didn't have any news to give me. After lunch on the Monday, I was told that they had found Mum at home, and that a member of staff had gone to collect her in the minibus. They said it would be an hour or so. I gathered up Sally, Richard and Jeffrey and walked down the long driveway right to the end. We sat there waiting for about two or three hours. Eventually, the minibus appeared, coming around the corner; sitting in the front seat with the driver were both Mum and Dad. The minibus did not stop to pick us up, so we all hurried back up the long driveway to the house. Mum said nothing about her running away, but it was a relief to have her back. That night, Dad also stayed with us at Forth House.

Next morning, Dad told me that we were all going back home. Some of the staff came while we were in the dining room having our breakfast and packed up our belongings.

I was pleased to hear the news, as I would be able to see my friends again and go back to my old school. After breakfast, we all got in the minibus and travelled back home.

CHAPTER 7

"Mum's Breakdown"

About three weeks of the summer holidays remained, before the return to school. I spent much of this time playing with my friend, and others from her family. My sister and brothers usually came along too. We went to the water meadows to have fun, sometimes bathing in the river or going for long walks up nearby hills. One of these hills had a maze right at the top, and we enjoyed playing in it. September arrived; time to go back to school. It was good to see other friends again, and Sally was also there with me. Richard was not due to start at this school until the following spring. By early October, Mum was becoming more and more mentally ill. She started coming up to my bedroom late at night, when I was already in bed. She would wake me up, sit on the end of my bed, and talk at me non-stop, about her childhood and all the things that had happened to her. At first she would do this two or three times a week, but soon it started to happen virtually every night. She would sit there on my bed for hours at a time, talking. If I tried to close my eyes, she would thump my arm with her fist and behave aggressively towards me. It felt like being crushed under a huge weight; the constant pressure was too much for me to cope with. Inside my head I wanted to scream at her "leave me alone", but I didn't dare. I had to keep it all bottled in. One night, while Mum was still downstairs, I crept down the stairs to get a drink of water. I reached the bottom of the stairs when suddenly Mum leaped out from inside the kitchen and grabbed hold of me, her hands around my throat. She kept her hands round my throat for what seemed to me like nearly a minute, all the time muttering that I was an intruder. I was too shocked to be able to do anything, and I was slowly choking. Then suddenly, her facial expression changed. She started to tell me I was an angel, sent from God, and that she must let me live.

During this period, Mum would try to boil the kettle or cook things in a saucepan without putting in any water. She would often be muttering that the devil was out to get her. "Can you hear him?" she would ask me. "He's behind me; he's trying to kill me."

She would become highly agitated, moving around the house and garden at much greater speed than was usual for her.

"Get away from me you devil, leave me alone," she would say, looking behind her with great anxiety. "You can't have me; Go away!"

I was becoming exhausted due to these things that were happening in the house. Mum's nightly visits to my bedroom continued; each night she repeated the same things to me, until I got to know it all by heart. But she never seemed to expect answers from me. I was kept awake for hours every night, but still had to go to school in the morning. On one occasion, Mum woke us all up at about five o'clock in the morning. She made us all get dressed for school. (I also used to help Richard and Jeffrey to dress). I kept telling her that it was much too early to go to school, but she wouldn't listen. She pushed Sally and I out of the house, but the boys stayed at home. Sally and I were forced to wait in the school playground, alone in the dark and freezing cold. Eventually, some other people began to arrive.

About this same period, one of my school friends spoke to me about a children's club, just up the road. It was called the "Lighthouse," and it met after school every Monday for about two hours. The club was run in a little "Free Evangelical" church, which was located at the far end of our road. Some students from the Christian Union at the local Teacher-Training College ran this club, to reach out to children from poor families in the area. I decided to go along there with my sister and brothers, and my school friend.

They would start with some songs, played with piano and guitars, and I liked to sing along and clap, jump, stamp my feet and join in with the actions. Then they would have a Bible story, using pieces of felt to make figures on a board. We would also do crafts, making things to take home; and they would sometimes play something called "draw swords:" The first person to find a particular verse in the Bible would win a prize. I found I really enjoyed going along to this club.

At about this time, I started to have a recurring dream. I found this dream very unpleasant. In it, the road outside our house turned into an old cobbled street. It was pitch dark with no streetlights; a man leading a horse and cart came along and stopped right outside our house. This man was dressed in a long black cloak and hood, so that I could not see his face. I could actually hear the clip-clopping sound of the horses' hooves on the cobble-stones. The man would come to our door and knock. I would answer the door, dressed in a long white robe. Then the man would point at the cart. On the back of it was an empty coffin.

"I have come to take your mother;" he would say, grimly. "No! You can't have her." I would reply. "Go away and leave us alone!"

I would shut the door; then I would wake up from the dream feeling very frightened. One day, the doctor had made a visit to our house. He made a suggestion to Dad.

"If your wife thinks that she is always seeing the devil in the mirror," the doctor said, "maybe you should put an angel on your kitchen mirror."

I overheard this conversation. I decided, while at the Lighthouse, to make lots of angels out of cardboard. Then I painted them all white, and I attached a string to each one. I took the angels home and hung one on the bottom of every bed, and one on every mirror I could find in our house. I thought this might help Mum. At first, she objected to the angels, but she couldn't touch them, because she was scared of them. She wouldn't go near any mirror to look at herself because of the angels; she kept pleading with me to take them down, but I refused.

It was school half term, and Johnny was due to come and spend a week with us at home. When he arrived, he was still full of energy, wanting to play games, mostly with me. But I wasn't up to his games. I was already very tired from being kept awake at night and from having to take care of the others. About three days after Johnny arrived, in the middle of the night, Mum came in and sat on my bed as she usually did, talking at me. She had a full bottle of undiluted orange squash in one hand. In her other hand, unnoticed by me, she held a bottle of tablets, which had been prescribed by the doctor. After an hour or two of talking at me, she suddenly stopped. She began to swallow the entire bottle-full of tablets right in front of my eyes; she was swallowing them down with the undiluted squash, straight from the bottle. Inside my head I had loud thoughts saying,

"Why is Mum drinking undiluted orange squash? Isn't that bad for her? It might make her very ill."

She had already drunk more than half the bottle. I jumped out of my bed and ran down the stairs to Dad's bedroom. He had heard me coming. I said to him,

"Mum is drinking undiluted orange squash and swallowing all her tablets, in my bedroom."

Dad didn't even try to get up from his bed.

"Well what do you expect me to do about it? He replied; "Go and fetch Mrs Beck from up the road. She'll sort her out!"

As usual with Dad, there were plenty of swear words added in as he spoke. I had to run up the road in my nightclothes, in the cold and dark; then I had to bang on Mrs Beck's door. It was about two o'clock in the morning. I had to keep banging for a few minutes until her oldest daughter came anxiously to the door, with Mrs Beck right behind her. Before they would open the door, they wanted to know who was there and what was the matter. I told them it was me, by speaking through their letterbox. Then they opened the door. I tried to explain what Mum had done, but I was in a state of panic and shock. Mrs Beck quickly got herself dressed and called an ambulance to our house. Then she hurried down the street with me to our house. By this time, Mum had made her way downstairs. She was now sitting on the sofa, looking very drowsy. Mum liked Mrs Beck, and tried to greet her, imagining that Mrs Beck was making a social call. Mrs Beck had to keep slapping Mum's face lightly, in order to keep her awake. She also tried to keep her talking. Very soon, an ambulance arrived. Now Dad appeared downstairs, followed by the rest of the family. Dad suddenly started to wail and sob. He was calling in a loud voice for his mother. Mrs Beck did not like him doing this in front of the family. She told him to sit down and calm down, and so did one of the ambulance men. They took Mum to the hospital in the ambulance, but Dad refused to go with her. Then Mrs Beck returned to her house, and we all went back to our beds. By now, Dad had stopped his wailing and moaning, and he also went back to his bed. Early the next morning, Dad went off to work as usual, leaving us on our own.

It was still quite early when a car pulled up outside our house, and someone knocked at our front door. I opened the door. There was a man standing there. He was the same man who had brought Johnny.

"I have come to take Johnny back because your Mum is unwell and she is unable to look after him;" he said.

Johnny had to go with him, but he was unhappy about it.

Later that same day, during the afternoon, we had a visit from five social workers, in four different cars. I opened the door and one of them said

"Hello, can we come in? We need to talk to you."

I let them come in, because I was worried about Mum. I thought they were coming to talk to us about her.

One of the ladies explained that she had found some nice people who loved children, and who wanted to take care of us while Mum was in hospital.

"Would you like to come in the cars to meet these nice people?" she asked.

The lady explained that she had found a nice family to look after Sally. She would have nice things and be taken care of there. There was also a nice family for Richard, and he would have lots of things to play with too. Then she said that there was a nice family waiting for me too, who would take good care of me.

"What about Jeffrey? I replied; "and what about my school. I don't want to go to a different school. I want to go to my own school."

"We also have a nice couple who would love to look after Jeffrey," they said.

"No!" I exclaimed. "Jeffrey is staying with me. You are not taking Jeffrey away from me. Otherwise I won't go anywhere with you."

They talked among themselves, and two of them left, taking Sally and Richard with them, both under a lot of protest. Three people stayed with me, and I had Jeffrey in my arms to try to protect him. The lady said that one person would go back to their office to make phone calls, to see if the family that was taking me would take Jeffrey too. She also said that they would see if I could stay at my school. We waited an hour or so until the person came back.

"Yes! This family have agreed to take Jeffrey as well. And you can stay at your old school."

I agreed to go with them. Jeffrey and I got into their car. As the car pulled away, I felt like I wanted to cry, but I couldn't let my feelings out in front of the social workers or Jeffrey. I swallowed my feelings down into my stomach.

CHAPTER 8

"Foster-Home"

We only travelled a very short distance in the car before arriving at our new foster-home. It turned out to be very near the house where we had lived before. The car stopped outside a house, and the two social workers got out. Then I also got out with Jeffrey; I was still holding his hand. I felt like I wanted to cry, but once again I swallowed it all down.

We were led to the house through a side gate and down a long path through the back garden. Mrs Miller, our new foster-mother, came to meet us at the back door of the house. She was quite short and stocky. First, she talked to the social workers that had brought us; then she looked at Jeffrey and me, smiled and said

"Hello! It's nice to meet you. Please come in and sit down." We obeyed, and were soon sitting on her sofa. She fetched us both a drink and some biscuits on a plate. At that very moment, a little black and white dog came running in, barking. Jeffrey was scared of it; but I liked dogs, so I started to talk to it. It came right over and sat at my feet and I started stroking it's head and back. This was comforting for me, as I have always been fond of dogs. Mrs Miller had now come back into the room, and seemed pleased that I liked her dog. She said his name was Dino. Then the social workers finished their drinks and left the house. Mrs Miller took us both on a tour of the house, to show us where we would be sleeping. Upstairs, there was a bedroom for Mrs Miller and her husband; there was a second bedroom for their three small sons to share, and a smaller bedroom for Jeffrey and me. I had a proper bed and Jeffrey had a camping bed. There was also a bathroom upstairs. Downstairs, they had a living room, a dining room and a kitchen. There was a T.V. in the living room, which I would enjoy watching.

About an hour or so after we had arrived there, a neighbour came in with some clothes for me to wear; Jeffrey and I had arrived with only the clothes we had on. Also accompanying this neighbour were Mrs Miller's three sons: Peter was five years old; Mark was three and John was two. I found it rather overwhelming to meet all these new faces, and then to my embarrassment, I was asked to try on the clothes that the neighbour had brought round, in front of everybody. Anyway, the clothes did fit me, and they were nicer than my usual clothes. Meanwhile, Jeffrey took a liking to the two older boys and they all started to play with toys on the floor. A short time after this, Mr Miller arrived back from his work. I liked him straight away, because he was very friendly to me and smiled a lot. He talked to me in a very kind, caring and gentle manner. This eased the fear and anxiety that I was feeling, and now I didn't have so much dread about staying with them.

Jeffrey and I spent the next four months living with this family. We were looked after much better than we had been at home. We had regular meals and baths, and even my school-friends started to say how much cleaner I looked. I liked Mr Miller and would sometimes watch "Westerns" with him on the television. These were films about "Cowboys" and "Indians", and I would annoy him with my constant questions about what was happening in the film, which he would graciously answer. I was not so well at ease with Mrs Miller. She would sometimes shout orders, because she had several children to cope with, and I found that any shouting would frighten me. I didn't spend a lot of time with her, as I was often outside, playing with the neighbourhood children. Mrs Miller was always happy for me to walk Dino, so I used to do this a lot. During the evenings, I would usually be indoors watching television. During the Easter break, we all went on a family outing to the seaside. I had never seen the sea before, or the beach. We played on the beach and made sandcastles. Then we ate jam sandwiches with bits of sand in them, but we didn't paddle or swim in the sea, as it was still too cold. Jeffrey and I really enjoyed this outing. We had some other days out that Easter, but these were to the park or to the shops.

One Saturday, I asked if I could take Dino for a walk, and Mrs Miller agreed as usual. I had been worrying for some time about Mum, wondering if she was back from hospital. I knew the way to our house as it was just over the road from the school I attended, but I had never tried to make a visit after school. But now I made the twenty-minute walk to our house, intending just to look through a window to see if I could see Mum inside. When I reached the house, I noticed that the door at the bottom of the steps, leading to the basement, had been left wide open. I crept down the steps very gingerly, and peeped round the door. I saw Dad lying completely still and silent on the floor at the bottom of the stairs. He must have been painting a ceiling with the help of a stepladder, as this was still standing at the top of the stairs. I took one look at him lying there and ran up the road with Dino as fast as I could to Mrs Beck's house. Luckily, her front door was open, so I shouted to her from outside.

"Dad is lying at the bottom of the stairs and he won't wake up. I think he's hurt himself."

She came quickly out of her house and said

"Hello Maureen, nice to see you. You do look well cared for and so much cleaner. How are you doing?" Then she added, "Don't worry, I'll take care of your Dad. You go on back with that little dog to where you're supposed to be."

I hurried back to my foster-home with Dino. Mr and Mrs Miller never knew where I had been that day. Within a month or so, social workers came unexpectedly to our foster-home after school, and told us that we were now going back to our own home. I hardly even had time to say goodbye, especially to Mr Miller, as he was at work. Jeffrey and I got into their car with our bags, which had already been packed, and in a few minutes we found ourselves back at home again.

At first I missed being with the foster-family, but I soon got back to my old routine, caring for Jeffrey, which I had not really been able to do at the foster-home. Within the next day or two, Richard and Sally also arrived home. Richard had been on holiday with his foster-family, to the Channel Islands, and he had brought back a photograph of himself with them. But Sally was very quiet about her foster-family and never talked about them. Meanwhile, Mum had already been home from hospital for about two weeks before we all came back. However, once all the family were back home again, she soon started to become agitated once again. Fortunately Dad seemed to be no worse for wear after his fall a month before, but he never mentioned it.

A month later, the summer holidays had just started, when Johnny came home, much to my surprise. Apparently he was due to spend some time with us all during the holidays. However, by this time, Mum was getting very ill again. For about two weeks already she had been keeping me awake again at night, sitting on the bed and talking at me, just like she had done before. This time I had just turned ten years old. Only a day or two after Johnny had come home, Mum was in the kitchen. Out of the blue she asked me, "Did you like it better being at that foster-home or being here?"

I was distracted at that moment, doing something with Jeffrey, and I replied; "The foster-home."

Immediately after I had said this, I knew inside that this was not the answer that Mum needed to hear, even though it was the truth. Later on that day, at teatime, all the family were gathered round a table in the sitting room. Mum was standing up, pouring a cup of tea for her and for Dad. Without warning, she suddenly collapsed in a heap on the floor, as though she was dead. Jeffrey started to scream at the top of his voice, and I froze in shock. Johnny, Richard and Sally reacted by running out of the house and up the road to the alleyway. Meanwhile, the teapot had fallen and smashed on the floor, spilling hot tea over the carpet. Then Dad yelled at me.

"Go and get Mrs Beck!"

I ran as fast as I could up to her house with my heart racing, and banged loudly on her door. Mrs Beck came hurrying to her front door.

"Whatever's the matter, Maureen?" She asked.

"Quick!" I said, all out of breath, "Mum has fainted onto the floor and we can't wake her up."

Mrs Beck quickly told her oldest daughter to phone for an ambulance, and then ran with me down the road to our house. Once inside, she went immediately over to Mum, who was still lying motionless on the floor, and started throwing Mum around to try to make her sick. Mum was not breathing.

While Mrs Beck was doing this, she shouted across to Dad, "Take Jeffrey out of the room!"

Little Jeffrey was still screaming, and was very distressed. But instead, Dad just sat there crying and wailing, calling for his mother. He was saying

"Mum, you can't leave me, you can't go."

Mrs Beck was furious with him, and so I had to take Jeffrey by the hand and lead him outside to the road. At this moment, an ambulance, with lights flashing, came speeding up the road to our house. Meanwhile, as if by a miracle, Mrs Beck had succeeded in getting Mum to be sick, and Mum had started to breath again. Mum was carried on a stretcher into the waiting ambulance, which took her to the local hospital, with siren blaring and lights still flashing. I still felt shocked and dazed by this event.

On the same day, very soon after this, a car arrived to collect Johnny and take him back to wherever he had come from. The others were nowhere to be found, so Jeffrey and I with Mrs Beck all went looking for them. We found them hiding in someone's garden, and Mrs Beck and I brought them back. Then we had to say good-bye to Johnny once again, after a very brief stay. I felt very sad to see Johnny have to go away again so soon. Later that evening, Dad discovered that a whole bottle-full of his pills for bronchitis had all disappeared.

CHAPTER 9

"First Children's-Home"

Early the next morning, a social worker driving a Mini pulled up outside our house, just a few minutes after Dad had left for work. This social worker had not been to our house before. He wanted all four of us to get into his car, saying that he was going to take us to a big house where there were also other children, so that we could all have a nice holiday. Straight away, I took a dislike to this man, because of his appearance and his manner. I decided that I could not really trust him. However, we all had to get into his small car, and Jeffrey had to sit on my lap in the back. Once again, I was forced to swallow down all the emotions I was feeling; I had to be strong for the sake of the others. The journey took about forty-five minutes, but eventually we reached a long driveway leading up to a big house, though not as big as Forth House had been.

This house had very large grounds, with a lawn, trees with ropes for swinging, a climbing frame and slide and other children's toys, bikes, scooters, etc. There were children playing all over the front lawn as we arrived, and all this should have looked inviting to us. Even so, I did not feel excited. Instead, I felt very alone, afraid and upset inside. Sally, Richard and Jeffrey also stayed very quiet as we were arriving. We all piled out of the Mini and were taken inside by the social worker, where we were introduced to two ladies. They told us their names, and how we were to refer to them; then they took all of us straight to the washrooms. They forced each of us to take a bath, during which we had to be scrubbed by a lady. This was embarrassing and humiliating, and made us feel very dirty. I was ten years old now, and I didn't like to be scrubbed like a small child. After this, they took away all our clothes, and supplied us with new ones. After all this, we were shown around the house. Downstairs they had a big lounge, a dining room and kitchen, but this was out of bounds. Upstairs there were girls' dormitories at one end of the house, and boys' dormitories at the other end. This meant that Sally and I had to be separated from Richard and Jeffrey. The staff members seemed very strict and scary; I didn't like them much at all. I couldn't make a fuss about Jeffrey, even though I didn't want him taken away from me at night. The ladies spelt out all the house-rules as they were showing us around the house. These rules were very strict and must be obeyed; otherwise there would be punishments to face. We were to stay in this place for six weeks, which was the remaining part of the summer holidays.

Soon after our arrival, I noticed another girl of about my age. She had brown skin, and she had two younger brothers similar in age to Richard and Jeffrey. She slept in my dormitory, so I started to talk to her at bedtime. I felt sorry for her because she and her brothers were being called rude names because of their skin colour. They were left out of all games and activities, and none of the other children played with them or talked to them. Because I started to talk and play with the girl, and my brothers played with her brothers, we started to get treated just like her and her brothers. I felt isolated and lonely, because all the other children turned against us, calling us rude names. I would go out cycling with my new friend, round the nearby country lanes, to get away from the house and grounds and the other children. We would pretend that we didn't really live in that children's home, that we were really sisters and that we had a nice family to go home to. Once back at the big house, we did get to swing sometimes on the ropes in the garden, but only when the other children were all occupied elsewhere.

I only remember going on one outing, which was to the seaside. It was a long drive from the children's home, but the weather was warm, and some of the children paddled in the water and built sandcastles, while older children like me were allowed to swim in the sea. I had recently learnt to swim at school, so I was not afraid to go in. This was the first time that I had swum in the sea, and I enjoyed it very much. Later, we were allowed on some rides at the fairground, and I had my friend with me. On the way home, the two minibuses stopped, and the staff bought fish and chips, which we all ate inside the buses. This was the best day of our stay at this home.

Now the time had come for us to go back to our own home. I had only been told that we were going home just a day or two before we left the big house. I had to try to tell my friend that I was going home with my brothers. When I did so, she got very upset; she tried desperately to cling onto me.

"Don't leave me! You can't go! What am I going to do without you? I may never see you again."

These were some of the things she said to me as she clung helplessly to my arm. It made me feel so unhappy and guilty, as I didn't want to leave her behind. I just didn't know what to say to her, as everything that was happening was outside my control. I think I said,

"Maybe one day we'll see each other again."

But in fact we never did.

The next day, the time came for us to go. I was happy to be going home, but sad to be leaving my friend. She had just re-started at school that morning, so I was unable to say goodbye to her. The same social worker with his Mini took us all back home. Mum had returned home by now, but she still didn't seem very well to me. We were happy to be back home, but there was no real emotion shown or greeting given us. Instead Mum just said

"Oh Hello; you're back then?"

I was left to bring in the bags and unpack them all. Later on, Dad came back from his work. He acted as if nothing had changed, as if we weren't even there.

The following day, we all returned to school, all except for Jeffrey, who was starting preschool. I was happy to see some of my friends again, and to catch up on what others had done during the summer holidays. I also started to attend the "Lighthouse" once again, together with my family and one or two of my friends. Unfortunately one or two of the girls and boys who were my friends at school, began to mess around and be rude; sadly I would sometimes join in with them. We would often annoy the pastor of the little church and in exasperation, he would tell us to get out of the building. Actually I hated being thrown out because I enjoyed being there; it used to make me feel bad inside. Fortunately they would always let us in again the following week, and no one was banned permanently. Gradually I learned to avoid joining in with the others when they were messing around, as I did not want to miss the meeting.

It was now Winter and Christmas came and went, but as usual this meant just one present for each of us, together with a stocking containing a few chocolates, sweets and a fruit. We had no Christmas tree or lights at home, but we did have some paper chains hanging across the ceiling, which Mum would struggle to put up. On Christmas Day we used to have a roast chicken instead of a turkey. This year somebody had given us a hamper, so there were some welcome extra treats. New Year passed, and as spring approached, Mum was becoming more ill again. She began coming to my room again at night, doing all the same things as before, especially talking at me for hours on end. This made me feel overwhelmed and I would get a crushing feeling inside my head. On top of this, when she became like ill, I was also expected to take on more responsibility for Richard and Jeffrey. When I wasn't at school, I would like to spend time away from the house in places like the local park, and I would take Sally and the boys with me. Mum had been ill for several weeks without any visit from a doctor. One early evening, she was in the kitchen. Suddenly she started to scream and howl, crying out for her mother in a hysterical voice.

This terrified Sally, Richard and Jeffrey. But me; I just felt numb inside. I was trying to think.

"What do I do? Do I fetch Mrs Beck again?"

Meanwhile Dad, who had not yet left for the pub, was no help to me at all. He sat on his chair in the living room, swearing and shouting at her to shut up. All this went on for what seemed like an hour or so; then Dad got up abruptly out of his chair and walked out of the house heading for the pub. Mum was still screaming and crying. I asked Sally to keep an eye on the other two while I ran up the road to Mrs Beck's house. Amazingly, she was at home once again, and soon she was hurrying back with me to see Mum. Mrs Beck quickly decided to call an ambulance because Mum was not responding to the fact that she was there. The ambulance arrived after only a few minutes. Out from the back came two men wearing white coats, who hurried into the kitchen. They took hold of Mum and placed a "straight jacket" on her, which was then strapped to a special chair, which they had fetched. Mum was carried out to the ambulance, still screaming and crying for her mother. We witnessed all this, and it made me say to myself,

"I must never cry or scream, because if I do, I will get carried off to hospital just like Mum"

This reinforced the fear that I already had of crying or showing emotion. Meanwhile, Mrs Beck had sent some-one to the pub with a message asking for George to go home and take care of his family. We went to bed, shaken and scared; finally Dad arrived home very late. He had drunk too much.

The following day, we received a visit from two ladies with a car. At first, I assumed that they were more social workers, coming to take us away again. But they said no; they were "Home-Helps." They came by after school and gave us baths. They had to boil up many saucepans of water on the cooker, and then carry them all the way upstairs to the bathroom. They also cooked some food for us, and they tried to clean the house; but it was beyond cleaning. The ladies also took our clothes away to be washed and then brought them back again, cleaned and ironed. At the weekend, one of the ladies took Sally and Richard to her home for the weekend, while the other lady visited Jeffrey and me. Then, the next weekend Jeffrey and I went for a weekend, while the other lady came to visit Richard and Sally at home. This continued for the six weeks that Mum was in hospital.

During the period that Mum was away, we were taken on three separate occasions to visit Mum in hospital. After school, the social worker with the Mini arrived to collect Dad and all four of us kids, to make the half hour journey to the hospital. It was a real squash in his little car. The hospital was very big, with lots of different buildings. Mum was on a ward with many other people of different ages. It was scary for us because the people were all mentally ill; they would shout, laugh, cry or make strange faces, comments and noises. I found this a rather frightening experience, as I already hated hospitals. On the first visit, Mum was agitated, rocking backwards and forwards on a chair. She ignored us, as if we weren't even there. This made me feel very rejected and upset inside. I said to myself

"I will never go to somewhere like this, and I never want to be like Mum."

By the last visit, Mum had got quite a bit better, and she was now able to recognise and acknowledge us. She wanted to take us to the "Blue Room". This is a room where all the patients who are able to, meet to drink tea, smoke, play cards etc. The atmosphere was thick with cigarette smoke. There was one particular older gentleman who was comical. He acted like the "Lord of the Manor", making funny noises or laughs. The two boys nicknamed him Lord Haw-Haw. Richard and Jeffrey also poked fun and laughed at some of the other patients who had funny mannerisms. This was their way of coping with the situation. After each visit, the journey home would take much longer! This was because Dad would insist that the social worker stop his car at three different pubs on the route home. The four of us kids had to wait each time while the two men went in for a drink. We were very bored and fed up, having to wait outside in the car. By now, all we wanted was just to get back home.

CHAPTER 10

"Changing School"

Four months had now come and gone, during which Mum had been away in hospital. It was now early July when she finally arrived back from hospital. I didn't see her come home because I was at school. When I did get home, she was there. To me she seemed rather drowsy, yet she was also very twitchy and shaky. When she tried to pick up a cup and saucer, her hand would shake so much that most of the tea spilled out into the saucer. She also seemed quiet and subdued, and I was thankful when she left me alone at bedtime. Now that Mum was back home with us, this meant that the two ladies, who had been helping us every day, didn't need to come anymore.

The summer holidays started in late July, so now we were all off school. I had just finished my last term at the Junior School, while Jeffrey was due to start at the same school that September. I spent much of the holiday period feeling very anxious about starting at the "big" school next term. I was worried about bigger kids picking on me and calling me nasty names. The school was also situated a long walking distance from our house. I had not made a visit there, so I had no idea what it would be like. I was very fearful about leaving my familiar surroundings, but I kept this inner sense of dread to myself for the whole of the holidays, and never spoke to anyone else about it.

During this holiday period, I spent most days taking my sister and brothers to the open-air swimming pool on the other side of the town. It would take half an hour to walk there and the same again to walk back. We would take our swimming costumes and two towels to share between us, which I would carry in a bag. We would paddle and swim and play in the shallow end water. We could sometimes join in with other children who were there, if they let us. On some occasions I had enough money to buy us all an ice-lolly, and on the walk home I would sometimes get given scraps for us to eat, by calling in at the fish and chip shop, or the greengrocer's shop for over-ripe fruit, which we would eat on the way home. These kindly shopkeepers knew who we were, and would always manage to find something to give us. Sometimes they even gave us items of food, which were not scraps or pieces to be thrown away. Of course, I did have to pay for the entrance tickets to the swimming pool and also for the ice-lollies, but I managed this because I used to run shopping errands for two different people. One of these was Mrs Beck; she would occasionally give me pocket money for going to the local shop for her, to buy some groceries. The other was a very old lady who lived three doors away from our house, and who always dressed in black. She wore clothes that resembled Victorian times. The local children were frightened of her because she would rap on her window with her walking stick if they made too much noise, and shout at them, "Go away!" We used to wonder if she was a witch or something, because of her black clothes and her stick. One day, to my surprise, while we were playing nearby, she appeared on her doorstep carrying a shopping basket on one arm. She motioned with her other arm for one of us to come over to her. My friends were scared and ran off, but despite my fear, I approached her rather nervously, wondering what she was wanting. When I was close enough, she asked me if I could go to the grocery shop for her. It was about ten minutes walk away. She had written out a shopping list, which was placed inside the basket, together with a purse containing some money for the groceries. She also said that I could buy myself a chocolate bar, but just the one for myself. She insisted that I must go to the shop on my own, without all the others. I carried out this errand for her exactly as she had asked, and brought back all the items on her shopping list, with exactly the right amount of change inside her purse. She seemed very pleased, and then gave me a generous tip. So I continued to do errands for this lady over the summer months. If she saw me in the street nearby, she would often come out of her house with her basket. After the holidays were over, she even waited for me to come back from school on occasions, and asked me to do some more shopping for her.

During these summer holidays, we were also taken on an outing once a week by a voluntary group who were trying to help deprived children. They would collect all four of us, together with some other children from local families, and they would take us all out in a bus. One week, we visited an old castle, then a beauty spot another week. We also were taken on a trip to a beach at the seaside, where they brought food and drink for us all. I enjoyed these trips, but I was very protective of my sister and brothers. Because of the experiences that we had already been through, I did not let any of the volunteers come too close either to me, or to my family members.

The holidays had come to an end, and the day arrived for me to start at senior school. I was now eleven years old. The school was for girls only. My friends from junior school took the bus, but I had to walk, as I had no money for the bus-fare. I eventually reached the school, and all the first year "starters" had to go into the Main Hall together. I was amazed at how many girls there were; there must have been two hundred or more. I felt both nervous and shocked, at the same time. I found my friend Jenny from my old school, which was a comfort, but then I had another shock when the teacher put us in different tutor groups. Thankfully, we did get to meet up later in some of the classes. We were read the school rules, and then taken to our tutor rooms to receive out timetables. We were expected to find our way to the different classrooms and departments. It was all very overwhelming, and it took me a week or so to settle in. Thankfully, I did have some familiar faces from my old school in some of my lessons. As soon as the bell went at the end of the school day, I would leave as quickly as I could, and run most of the way home in order to be there when Sally, Richard and Jeffrey finished their school. It was mostly downhill from the school, so I could do it in just under fifteen minutes. I was worried that Mum would not be able to cope with the others after school without me around.

Sadly, Mum was now getting ill again, with all the usual symptoms. She was spending hours by my bedside late at night, and talking non-stop about her life experiences. I heard all the same stories so many times before, and I knew them off by heart. Nothing seemed to be done about her condition by Dad, and I was too busy coping with my new school and the others in the family. In addition to this, I was now having less sleep than usual.

One evening in October, during half term, Mum was standing in the kitchen, by the sink. Suddenly we heard a heavy thud as she had collapsed onto the floor, smashing the mug that was in her hand. I quickly ran from the living room into the kitchen, to find out what had happened. I saw Mum lying motionless on the floor, and I shouted to Dad. "Mum's passed out on the floor!"

Richard and Sally became agitated, and Jeffrey started running round in circles in a panic. He had been badly traumatised on the previous occasion when Mum had collapsed. Meanwhile, Dad stayed sitting in his chair as usual, and gave the expected command

"Go and get Mrs Beck!"

This was accompanied by some swear words. Once again, I ran up the road to her house, and thankfully she was at home. I told her what had just happened. Immediately, she asked one of her family to call for an ambulance, and she hurried down to our house with me. On the way there, she told me to fetch Jeffrey, Richard and Sally, and take them straight back to her house until the ambulance had been and gone. I obeyed her instructions, so I was not in the room at home to witness what actually happened. But I believe that she succeeded in bringing Mum back to life again. Meanwhile, the four of us children had gone back to Mrs Beck's house. Her son was there, and then she joined us a little later. She allowed us to stay with her for a couple of hours, and we were given some sandwiches and drinks, and watched television. Mrs Beck kept telling us that Mum would be all right, but that she would undoubtedly have to stay in hospital again, maybe for quite a while.

On this occasion, no social workers arrived at our house on the following day, unless they came when I was out in the park with Sally, Richard and Jeffrey. Dad carried on in his usual way, going to work by day and down to the pub by night. Then, on the second day after Mum had gone into hospital, we had some visitors arrive in the mid-afternoon. A little "three-wheeler" car pulled up, and two people got out of it. The driver was tall and dark haired, aged about in his forties. The woman was short and plump and quite a lot older. The man came down our steps to the basement asking, "Where's Joan, where's Joan?"

The way he spoke sounded very strange to me. I couldn't understand much of what he was saying, and he couldn't seem to understand me either when I tried to speak to him. Meanwhile the older woman had followed us inside, and she looked at us and announced

"I am Joan's mother, so I am also your grandmother. This is your Uncle Norman, Joan's brother. He can't hear you or speak very well because he is deaf and dumb. We have come to see Joan, your Mum. Where is she; is she at home?"

"No she isn't", I replied, "she is in hospital."

Then I explained what had recently happened.

"Then where's that father of yours?" the woman then asked, in a sarcastic tone of voice. "Is he in?"

"No, he's at work" I replied again.

"What!" she exclaimed. "So who is looking after all of you then?"

"I am," I said.

"It shouldn't be allowed," she exclaimed. "Well, we will come in and we will wait for your Dad to come home from work. We will have to sort some things out, and then we will visit Joan in hospital tomorrow."

My grandmother came in with her son Norman, and made herself as much at home as she could in our house. We also came back into the house and played games with Norman. We did not like the old lady because she was very bossy, but we did like Norman because he was very childlike, and gave rides to the boys on his back. After quite a while, we heard Dad's footsteps coming down the steps to our front door.

When he came in, he was most surprised to see Mum's relatives there, as they had travelled a long distance. However, he had no proper greeting for them. He just said; "She's not here. She's in hospital."

Meanwhile, grandmother, unperturbed by Dad's fobbing off tactics, began questioning him as to why he had been out at work, leaving his children unattended? What was he thinking about? Had he no sense of responsibility? Was he that stupid?

"It's your fault that my Joan is in hospital;" she then added to her other accusations. Dad swore and muttered under his breath. Then he tried to change the subject, by telling filthy jokes. When this tactic also failed, Dad then announced that he was going down to the "chippie" to get fish and chips for everybody! This was something he had never done before! Dad actually did come back with the fish and chips, and he handed them to me at the front door. Dad then told me that he was going out for the evening because he couldn't stand the "old *****". So off he went to the pub, even before normal opening time. My grandmother was furious when she realised that Dad had abandoned us all. Meanwhile, we spent the evening with her and with Norman, who continued to play games with us as best he was able. Grandmother sat all evening in a huff. We had no television, so she had nothing to do, and she didn't enjoy the noisy games that we were playing with Norman. Later on, at bedtime, she helped herself to Dad's bed, and she put Norman in the spare bed in Richard's room which was kept for Johnny's visits. The rest of us slept in our usual places. When Dad eventually came back after closing time at the pub, he found his bed occupied, and had to sleep downstairs in his armchair. Once again he was up and gone to his work before anybody else was up and about.

In the morning, grandmother and Norman got up and ate whatever they could find for breakfast. She told us that we would be going to visit Mum in hospital during the afternoon, but that first she had to go into town with Norman to sort out some things, like she had said before. Before they drove off, Norman gave each of us a one-pound note to buy a toy for ourselves, and some sweets. This was a lot of money for us in those days. Our two relatives drove off in their funny car with three wheels, but they never came back to take us to the hospital to visit Mum. I felt hurt and upset because I was looking forward to seeing Mum. I also thought Mum would be very happy to see her own mother and brother, especially as she had been calling for her when she was ill.

CHAPTER 11

"Oak Hall"

Grandmother and Norman had only been gone a few hours, when another car pulled up outside our house. There was just one person inside this car. He wasn't the same social worker that had taken us to visit Mum a few times. He came to our door and knocked; when I opened it, he introduced himself. He asked all four of us to get into his car, saying that we were going on a short journey. I had been expecting to visit Mum in hospital and already felt numb and upset, so this visit had come right out of the blue.

"Where are we going?" I asked the man; "and where are you taking us?"

"You are all going to a big house, which is called Oak Hall", he replied; "where you can stay while your Mum is in hospital. It is just nearby, so you will all be able to go to your present schools."

Dad was still at work, so Sally and I had to hurriedly gather together a few bits and pieces for us all to take with us, and Richard and Jeffrey brought with them the toys that they had just bought that day, with Norman's gift. The journey took only a few minutes in the man's car. It would have taken me about fifteen minutes on foot. We came to a driveway with a big gate, which was shut. Somebody came out quickly to open the gate and let us in, and our car pulled up in front of the house. We all got out with our belongings, and the people in charge met us in the hallway. Then the social worker left in his car. The woman who had come out to meet us introduced herself and her husband, and they then showed us around the house. Downstairs, there was a large living room, which was situated to the right of the hallway. It contained lots of chairs, one or two tables and a television. On the other side of the hallway was an equally large dining room. It had several tables, with a few chairs around each one. There was a staircase going up from the centre of the hallway, and to the left of this, a long corridor led off to the kitchens. These were out of bounds to the children, unless you were on washing-up duty. Finally, leading off the hallway on the other side was a passageway down to a big playroom, containing a table, a record player and boxes filled with all sorts of toys, games and puzzles. Next, we were taken upstairs, where we were shown our sleeping accommodation. I was upset to be told that Richard and Jeffrey were to sleep in the "Boys Wing", and Sally and I in the "Girls Wing," and that the girls were not allowed into the boy's wing. I was still very protective towards Jeffrey. He had been sleeping in my bed at home, and had been having recurring nightmares about Mum being taken off in ambulances. He had developed a great fear of ambulance sirens. So I had decided it was my job to be there for him at night times. But now I had to obey, as the lady was very strict; so Sally and I were shown our room. We would have to share this large bedroom with about six other girls of different ages. I did not like the atmosphere of this place very much. The lady in charge would force you to look her in the eyes when she spoke to you. She would get annoyed if you couldn't do this, and she would keep asking you to look at her this way. I hated to do this and found it very difficult, because it made me feel threatened and exposed. Inside I wanted to hide and run away. I had never been used to looking at anyone this way, and it felt to me like I was being told off or punished for doing something wrong.

I was able to walk to school from Oak Hall, so I still met up with some of my old school-friends at the senior school. I felt very upset because I wasn't allowed to go to the "Lighthouse" with my friends. I had so enjoyed those weekly meetings. However, I was still able to attend the St John's Ambulance Brigade, to learn First-Aid. I had started doing this when I was nine, and I enjoyed learning how to treat people for minor injuries. It made me feel better to know that I was trying to help others. Meanwhile, I was starting to struggle badly at school. I had so much pain and hurt inside me that I had become rude towards some of the teachers. My friend, Jenny and I would often mess around in classes, talking, laughing and telling jokes. We would call the teachers by silly names and be disrespectful to them. On one particular day, Jenny and I, together with two girls from Oak Hall, took some bicycles from the bike-sheds, and started riding them round the school grounds during lessons. Some teachers had to come out to round us up, and we were all suspended for a week. Someone from Oak Hall had to come to collect the two girls and myself, and on arrival back at the home, we were issued with punishments. I was made to sit for the whole day in the boiler-room, except for meal times. This continued for a whole week, and I found it really boring. I am not sure that this punishment taught me anything. I just hated the place and myself even more than ever. When I returned to the school after the week away, I was told that I had been separated from my friend Jenny. I had actually been moved up a grade in some subjects, and she had been moved down.

At Oak Hall, I could not seem to make any real friends. Different children there kept coming and going. I did manage to make friends with one girl, whose name was Donna. Then she had to move on somewhere else in the late autumn. When the weather was fine, most of the children would play outside. I used to like to organise the games, and tell the younger children what to do. One of my favourite games was driving downhill in a wooden cart, which was fitted with wheels, and I would often have two or three younger children riding on the back of the cart. Then, as the winter months came on, we would play games in the playroom and dance to music from the record player. When Christmas arrived, the four of us stayed on at Oak Hall. All the other children went to family or friends for Christmas, except for one boy of Richard's age, who stayed behind with us. Most of the staff had gone home for Christmas, but the lady in charge had some relatives visiting. They helped to look after us together with her husband. We didn't normally see much of him, as it was his wife who seemed to run the home. Over Christmas week, we had our meals in the playroom with all these new people. They were mainly couples, but there were no other children. On Christmas morning, there was a big surprise in store for us. We were each given a large bag containing presents, which we eagerly opened. I had never before received presents that were wrapped in pretty paper with bows and tags, and I found it quite overwhelming. The best present I received this Christmas was a watch. I was also given a diary, some make-up, a brush, a comb and some soap. The others too were very excited about their presents. The atmosphere was much happier than usual, and some of the adults got a little merry from Christmas cheer. I was allowed to join in with a game called "Cluedo" and also with various card games, which I really enjoyed. I also tucked in to the Christmas food, of which there was plenty to eat. And yet, deep down, I felt sad and home-sick; I couldn't help thinking about Mum. I had received no news about her since we had first come to the home, so I didn't know whether she was still in hospital or not. The Christmas holidays came to an end, and the other children came back to Oak Hall. The atmosphere soon returned to how it had been before. Now it was time to go back to school.

There was a teacher at the school who was not popular with any of the other girls. She always wore long dark-coloured dresses or skirts, and she had an abrupt way of speaking to people. This made her appear to be strict, old fashioned and unapproachable. I happened to be placed in her "Tutor Group." At this time I was still rude to teachers, behaving as I pleased, even though, deep down, I really wanted to please others and be appreciated. One Friday, I had arrived back at Oak Hall after school, when a member of staff informed me that I was going out the next day, a Saturday, to spend the day at my tutor's house. I was told that she would be collecting me at ten o'clock in the morning. I was very surprised, but I did not refuse, even though I wondered why she had asked me. Ten o'clock came, and my tutor duly arrived. There was no sign of any car, and it turned out that she did not have a car of her own. Instead, she had taken a bus to the bus station, and had walked all the way up the hill to Oak Hall. We walked together to the bus station, and caught a bus to her house. She actually lived very near to the school. I felt quite nervous on the walk and also on the bus, so there was not much conversation between us. But when we arrived at her house, there were two teenage boys in her kitchen. These were her sons, and I felt even more uncomfortable to be there. I was given a little snack and a drink, and the teacher asked me if I liked dogs. I said that I did, so then she let her Labrador dog into the kitchen from the garden. I began to feel much better as I stroked and petted her friendly dog. I have always liked dogs and they help to calm my nerves. Later that day, we had lunch together, and she asked me if I would like to go for a walk with her and the dog. I eagerly said, "yes", as I preferred to be outdoors than in, and I was feeling a little bored. The teacher led the way to the golf course, where she let her dog off the lead to run freely. Then she began to ask me lots of questions about my family; I did my best to answer them. She seemed very different to how she was at school. She was more approachable and seemed kind and caring towards me. She was even wearing more brightly coloured clothes. She seemed to be trying to find out whether I would like to go to live with her and her family. But I explained that I couldn't be separated from the others, and especially not from Jeffrey, because they needed me. She accepted my answers calmly, and did not try to argue with me. After the walk, I stayed on for supper; by this time her husband had come home from his work. After supper, he took me back to "Oak Hall" in his car. After this day-out, my behaviour towards this teacher improved greatly. I was no longer rude to her, and I even came to her defence once or twice when others were being disrespectful to her.

Some weeks later, on a Sunday afternoon, Mum came to Oak Hall to visit us. We had no warning of this visit, and possibly she had just decided to walk up from our home. The staff allowed her to come in, and even gave her sandwiches and tea. Jeffrey was very excited to see her. I too was very relieved to see that she was all right, yet I felt very distant from her. She seemed a lot better, and she was no longer doing any odd behaviour. After about an hour and a half, she left again to return home. I was beginning to experience times of "blackness" inside. I would get burning pains in my stomach and a deep pain within. I started to repeat over to myself

"I never want to be like my Mum; I will never take overdoses with pills like she has; I will never ever go to a mental hospital like she has."

I would say these words over and over to myself, usually when walking to school and back. At the same time, some of the older girls at Oak Hall started to give me cigarettes, and they showed me how to smoke them. I immediately discovered that smoking numbed the pain inside and made life more bearable. I started off only smoking a few cigarettes, but as time went by, the number increased. During the next two months, Mum arrived every Sunday for tea, but Dad never once came to see us during the whole time we were there. Then one day, in late March, a Social Worker came to see us. He announced that they had found a new home for us to live in, and that it was near the sea. I felt very unhappy about this, because I just wanted to go back home. I also wanted to stay at my current school, and be near my friends. I felt like a caged animal. I thought about escaping and running home, but I couldn't leave Sally and the boys behind. I was dreading this move; I didn't understand why we couldn't just go home to Mum and Dad.

CHAPTER 12

"St Mary's"

Just a day or two later, we were told to pack up our belongings, as we were about to be moving on. The next morning came, and instead of going to school as usual, the social worker with the Mini arrived at Oak Hall to take us to our new home. I had not even had a chance to say goodbye to any of my friends at school, although they did know that I was due to leave soon, to go and live somewhere else. We started on the journey, which took over half an hour. It seemed a long way into unfamiliar places, and we were all very silent, wondering what might lie ahead. Yet again, I had to swallow down my emotions, wanting to be strong for my younger brothers and sister. We drove up a cul-de-sac, situated in a housing estate. The car came to a stop at the far end of the road, at a place where three houses had been turned into one bigger house. There was no big driveway, so the car stopped right outside on the road. We all got out, carrying our bags, and walked through a gate onto a short garden path, which took us to a door leading into the kitchen. The couple-in-charge had come out to meet us as we walked up the garden path to the rear door. The social worker introduced each of us by name, put our bags down in the dining room, and then left. The lady was very friendly and kind to us, and smiled at us a lot. Her husband, on the other hand, seemed distant and disinterested in us. He quickly returned to whatever he had been doing. As for ourselves, we all stayed very quiet, as if in shock. I was trying hard to keep my emotions at bay, and I didn't feel like having to answer any questions. I kept swallowing a lot as the lady was showing us around the downstairs rooms and the bedrooms. She was explaining lots of details, including plans for a shopping trip for clothes and details for starting a new school, but right then I couldn't cope with all of it, nor even take it in. All I wanted was to be left alone to sit somewhere quiet; I wanted to try to imagine that I was somewhere completely different. But I had to try to face reality. Sally and I were to share a bedroom, together with one other girl. She was a year younger than me, and had already been there a few weeks. Meanwhile a young member of staff showed Richard and Jeffrey to their room, which they were going to share with another boy. To our surprise, we learnt that this boy was also coming from Oak Hall, and he arrived later that same day. This meant that the three young boys all knew each other, which was good. We also found out that there were already four teenage boys living at this home.

The first night at this new home seemed very strange, but at least I had taken a liking to the lady in charge. In the morning we all got up and washed and dressed. We came down to the dining room and were given cereals for breakfast. Then the other children had to leave to go to their schools, but we didn't have a school to go to yet. Instead, we were taken in their minibus into the town, to go shopping. The other boy who had arrived from Oak Hall came too. I liked the experience of shopping for new clothes, both for school use and for casual wear, as I had never ever shopped for clothes before. I picked out a dress or two; a nightdress; a sweater or two; some skirts; some shoes for school and for home, and some new underwear. We all got new school uniforms as well, according to whichever schools we would be attending. I kept asking the lady in charge if all of this wasn't costing too much money? She said that it wasn't her own money they were spending. She said that the money came from Social Services. I didn't really understand her answer, but I accepted it. I felt much happier inside with these new clothes to wear. We were out nearly all day, so we all had lunch in town as well. When we got back to St Mary's, we put our new clothes away in our bedrooms, and were allowed to play until teatime. There was a large playroom, which had a record player, and various toys and games. Next to this room there was a lounge with chairs and a television. This room was not for playing in. It was just for reading and for watching television. Sometime that afternoon I do remember asking the lady where the sea was. I said that we had been told that we would be near the seaside. She explained that yes, there was a beach, but it was about three miles away, too far to walk to on your own. However, she said that we would make trips to the beach during the summer holidays. Although I was disappointed, I was still too anxious about starting a new school to be too upset about the beach.

After a few days, we had all started at our new schools. I discovered that my school was about four miles away, in the nearby town where we had been shopping. On the first day, I was taken there by minibus, and the lady in charge came with me. When I got there, I had quite a surprise. The buildings and layout of the school were identical to my previous school. But the staff, pupils and uniforms were completely different. This gave me a very strange feeling at first, but I got used to it. After this first day, I had to take a bus to the school by myself. The boys from the home had different schools to go to. In the afternoons, I caught the bus back again, but once I was used to the route, I would spend the bus money at the chip shop, and then walk all the way back. I liked to do this, as I could live for a while in a fantasy world and daydream, mostly about things I had seen on the T.V. Quite soon, I had made two friends at the new school. They were best friends with each other, so it caused some friction at times having me around as well. We would hang around, talk together and mess around in class. Sadly, I began to be rude and disruptive again, and I probably caused trouble for them both. Even so, one of these girls was allowed to visit me for tea at St Mary's, and I went to her house once and also went swimming with her and her Mum. The other girl also came to the St Mary's for tea. Her Dad took us both to a league football match, and another time to motorbike speedway racing. I didn't much like the football, and preferred the bike racing.

Meanwhile at St Mary's, relationships were rather strained. I didn't get on well with the other girl in our room, and we had fights and arguments at times. One of the boys living there, who was already sixteen, started to kick Richard, Jeffrey and the other boy in their room.

One day, this older boy asked me to "go out" with him. I replied that I would only go out with him if he left the smaller boys alone, and stopped bullying them. To my surprise, he actually did stop hurting them. To be frank, I didn't like him very much. I was still only twelve, and he was sixteen, but I did dance with him in the playroom to music from the record player. The staff members were very concerned that I should not be left alone with him, but in actual fact he behaved well towards me and never tried to abuse me in any way. Then, one day, I came back from school to find that he was nowhere to be found. I asked one of the staff members where he was; they said that he had left that day, and wouldn't be coming back again. I felt hurt and rejected by this, as he had not told me that he was leaving. I realised that I had enjoyed his friendship and his company, and that I would miss him. Just a few weeks later, there was another upset. The lady in charge and her husband explained to us all that they were leaving the home. I had the feeling that they didn't want to leave, but had to go for some reason. The following day they were gone. I had liked the lady in charge, and now I would never see her again. Later that day, the replacement couple arrived. Their names were Reg and May. I didn't take a liking to them, because they didn't show kindness or caring towards the children in the way that the first couple had done. They quickly put a stop to some of the activities that I used to enjoy, such as the Saturday morning Cinema, and the weekly swimming trip. Reg would speak negative and damaging words to me, and to many of the others. He treated us as if we were there in the children's home because we were like rubbish, and a drain on society; as if we were sent there because we had committed crimes. He would say things to us like:

"You'll never amount to any good." Or "You'll just end up in prison."

I began to think that I must really be a bad person. Sadly, the atmosphere of the home changed for the worse, and I started to feel unhappy and restless, wanting to run away. On top of this, I had not seen Mum for a long time, and was worrying about her. So I started to plan an escape.

I was talking it over at night with Sally, but the other girl in the room was also listening. I had to agree for her to come with us too, otherwise she would have told on us. We also planned to take Richard and Jeffrey, together with the other boy who had come from Oak Hall. I had worked out a complicated plan: Everybody would set out for their schools in the nearby village as usual, including those who were dropped off by minibus, and everybody would then double back to a meeting point in a farmers field outside the village. I even organised that everyone would have home clothes on under their school uniforms. I took a few carrier bags to put these uniforms into. I had been getting a lift to my school in the town by a neighbour who lived in the Close, whose daughter was in my class. On the day before we planned to escape, I told this man that I wasn't going to school, as I had a dentist appointment. The day arrived, and everything went according to plan. All six of us met up in the farmer's field and took off the school uniforms. I placed them in the bags, and left them in the field, hidden amongst the tall crops. I also left my own school bag. Then we walked along the lane to the main road, heading in the direction of home. I made the boys hide down a bank, while Sally and I, with the other girl, started to try to thumb a lift. Each time a car stopped, the boys would come running out of their hiding place, but the first two cars could not fit us all in. So we all stayed together and tried again, still with the boys in hiding, and the girls thumbing for a lift. Finally a lady stopped. She was by herself, and her car looked quite big. She looked surprised and shocked to see how many of us there were, but she managed to fit us all in. During the journey, she asked us a lot of questions, but I did all the speaking. I replied that we were trying to visit my Mum who was in hospital. She took us to the place where I requested to go, which was quite close to Mum and Dad's house. After getting out of her car, we played for a few minutes on the playing fields nearby, but I was desperate to get to the house. We got to the house, but there was nobody there. I felt really disappointed; I didn't know what to do. I decided to call at Mrs Beck's house. She answered the door, and let us in. She was very surprised to see us all, and she gave us some food and drink. Then, about half an hour later, I saw through her window a police van arriving. Before the police even reached the front door, Sally and I and the other girl had all run out of the back door, through the garden gate and up the alleyway outside. Two policemen chased after us, and caught Sally while she was still in the back garden. The other girl and I stopped at the end of the alleyway, and soon gave our-selves up. The three boys had not even tried to run at all. We all travelled in the van to the police station, and there we waited until the social worker with the Mini arrived to collect us. The boy and girl who were not part of my family were taken by another social worker. After lectures from the police, we were taken back to St Mary's. Reg put a stop to our pocket money, and commented that it was now clear that we were bad children.

This escape was the first of three. When we went inside on the second escape, we found Dad at home, and the police waiting for us in the sitting room. They had hidden their van around the corner, where we did not notice it. Dad told me that Mum was back in hospital. Once again we were all taken back to St Mary's, and we got no pocket money for the following week. On the third occasion, it was again a weekend, as it had been for the second escape, and we had been going into the village to spend our pocket money. However we had decided to escape like we had before and with the same six children. This time we reached my house and there was no sign anywhere of a police van. We peered through the basement window into the sitting room and Dad was sitting there in his usual armchair. I decided it was all clear to go in, but when we had all piled into the sitting room, suddenly three policemen appeared in the doorway! It seems they had been hiding in the kitchen, and so had come down the short passage to block off the sitting room door. Once again, we had to go to the police station and wait for social workers to take us back to St Mary's.

By this time I had been at St Mary's for over a year, and I had reached my thirteenth birthday. I didn't try to escape any more. However one Saturday, quite unexpectedly, while we were all having lunch, the social worker with the Mini arrived; he had Dad as his passenger. Dad had now retired from work, as he was sixty-five years old. Dad came bursting through the kitchen door, ahead of the social worker.

"Mum is dying! He shouted. "Mum is dying!" He shouted again; "She hasn't got much longer to live!"

I was completely shocked and stunned. Suddenly Jeffrey got out of his chair, started to scream at the top of his voice, and began running about all over the house. I jumped down from my place and chased after him, together with some members of the staff. Meanwhile, the social worker was trying to explain to the remaining staff and Sally and Richard, that it was not our mother who was dying but it was Dad's mother! Meanwhile, I managed to catch Jeffrey; then a staff member ran up to us and told us the true facts. Never the less, it took me a while to calm Jeffrey down and convince him that it was not Mum who was dying. Dad stayed an hour or so at St Mary's, but the staff and children had not been impressed by his actions. For me, it was a huge relief that it was his mother and not my Mum, as I had no relationship with his mother. She must have been over ninety years old by now.

Over the following year, I started to experience abusive behaviour from an older boy in the home on a regular basis. He was now the oldest boy in the home, at sixteen, and he had a room to himself, which was located right next to the room I shared. Nearly every night, at bedtime, he would wait in his room until I went to the bathroom to clean my teeth or visit the toilet. The bathroom door had no lock, so he could creep in and grab me from behind. Then he would hold me with his arms round my chest, and abuse me from behind whilst I stayed standing. I never screamed or called for help, though I used to tell him to leave me alone. I never reported him to the staff or to anyone else because I thought I should protect him, being another member of the same children's home. I was gradually becoming more disturbed at school. Some teachers became concerned about my behaviour and about the pain that I was suffering in my stomach area. I also experienced uncontrollable shaking episodes in my body lasting five minutes or so about three times per week. I never saw a doctor, but I did visit the Deputy Head teacher once a week for a talk. I was frightened of her, so I saw this more as a punishment than as help. By this time, I had little or no trust in any adult. My problems were set to continue without any solution for another year or so, but then another change was about to take place in my life.

CHAPTER 13

"Back home again"

At the end of July, as the summer holidays were starting and I had recently turned fourteen, I was given some unexpected news. Dad had asked for Sally and I to return home to help him, presumably with things like shopping and housework. This news stunned me! If I had to go back home, I didn't want to leave without Jeffrey! He often came running into my room at night for comfort after having a nightmare, and I felt he needed to have me around. During the last two or three months, I had become increasingly protective over Jeffrey, and I had even had a confrontation with a member of staff over him. During this incident, I had been pushed backwards, falling over and hitting my head, and I had then thrown a toy gun at her door, causing some damage to the door. Even though I was told that my Dad wanted me home, I had overheard conversations between the social worker and the person in charge of the home. These were suggesting that Jeffrey had to be separated from me, for his own good.

One morning, a few days later, Sally and I were told to pack our suitcases with our clothes and belongings. I had told Jeffrey and Richard that we were going home, and that they had to stay there a bit longer. Even so, Jeffrey could not accept this, and kept coming into my room with items of his clothing, trying to pack them in my suitcase. He was very distressed, and I felt very upset inside because I couldn't do anything about it. I wanted him to come with me, but I was trapped. Richard, on the other hand, did not seem to be bothered by our departure, at least not on the outside. Later that afternoon, the social worker with the Mini arrived to take Sally and I back home. He came in and picked up our suitcases to put in his car, while Sally and I were trying to say goodbye to everyone. Meanwhile Jeffrey was clinging onto me, gripping hold of my clothes, and as we tried to get into the car, he tried his utmost to get in with us.

"I'm coming too, don't leave me!" he screamed over and over again. In the end, a member of staff had to pull him away from us by force, so that we could drive safely away. Even so, Jeffrey managed to break free from her, and came running, screaming and crying down the road behind us, shouting over and over,

"Come back, come back, come back!"

I was torn apart inside. Feelings of anger and hatred filled my heart towards the social worker, and all the people in authority. Soon we went around the corner and Jeffrey disappeared from sight. I felt awful for the rest of the journey and I wasn't looking forward to getting home. Half an hour or so later, the Mini arrived at our house. Sally and I got out, and made our way inside with our suitcases. Dad and Mum were both at home, but there was only a brief "hello" and nothing more. However, there was a surprise in store. While we had been away for two years, Mum and Dad had got themselves a dog. Her name was Suzie, and she was probably a Labrador/Corgi crossbreed. She was still less than a year old, but already she had produced a litter of puppies, courtesy of the Red Setter who lived up the road. Dad had sold or given away all the females but had kept two males. One was black and smooth-coated like Suzie, and he had been given the name of Darkie; the other one was fluffy and red-coloured like a Setter. I fell in love with this puppy straight away, and I named him Donny. This was after Donny Osmond, who I liked at the time. In my emotions, I replaced Jeffrey with Donny, and took him with me everywhere I could. Two weeks later, we were allowed to go on a holiday with the staff and children from St Mary's, as this had already been booked for a long time. Sally and I went along, and of course we saw Richard and Jeffrey again. But even though I enjoyed myself and we had a good time, somehow the strong bond between Jeffrey and me seemed to have been broken. He seemed happy to be playing with the other boys, and no longer followed me around, clinging on to me. Over the next two or three years, I only saw Richard and Jeffrey a few times.

When the school holidays came to an end, I returned once again to the senior school, which I had attended two years earlier. Sally also started at this school for the first time. My former friend, Jenny, had made other friends by now, and she no longer wanted to talk to me at school. So I began to make friends with some of the girls with problems, many of which also lived in nearby roads to me. I myself was quite disturbed by now, and a doctor had prescribed sedatives to calm my nerves. I didn't take them all the time and I started to wander off from school more and more. One of my new friends, Jill, would usually wander off with me. As we had plenty of time on our hands and no money to spend, we started to get involved in petty crime. We shoplifted chocolate bars from "Woolworths", and once or twice were chased up the street by staff or other shoppers. We also made many visits to the Catholic Church in the centre of town, sometimes taking other girls with us. There was a big black box for worshippers to pay for candles which they would then light and place in candle holders. We would wait until the church was empty of people, then we would remove the remaining candles, and roll the box around until the money inside would fall out of the hole onto the floor. There was never a great deal of money, but it was a lot to us. I hated stealing really, but we often had no money or food at home because Dad had retired and was drinking in the pub most of the day and evening. He was spending all his pension money. I had to try to pay for food for the family and the dogs. I often bought tinned cat food for the dogs, as this was cheaper. It was only much later that I discovered that this was not good for them. Once a week, I was able to get scraps of meat from the butcher for my dogs.

During this year I met a social worker called Mrs Good. She had visited the house to take Sally and I to buy our school uniforms. Even though I had become very suspicious of adult authority figures, I sensed that she was a caring person, and after a while, I would sometimes visit the office where she worked, asking to see her. She wasn't always there, but often she was, and she always seemed willing and able to see me and talk to me. I began to see her as a friend, rather as I had done with Mrs Beck.

Over the next two years, Sally and I went with Mrs Good and other needy children, to social camp. This took place in a big house with grounds in the New Forest. We would spend a weekend away, which would include outings, walks, games and a cinema trip. I enjoyed getting away from home, because Mum was still unwell, going in and out of hospital regularly. I would recognise her symptoms developing, and call the Doctor whenever she was getting very ill. Then an ambulance would have to come and take her away.

During my last year of school, I had turned fifteen, and I had long golden-blond hair and blue eyes. I was of slim build, but with a woman's figure. I had begun to be pestered by much older men around the neighbourhood where we lived, offering me money for sexual favours. This may have also been because Dad had referred to me as a "prostitute" and a "bitch" ever since I was eight years old. These descriptions would have been heard in the pub, and although totally untrue, others were not to know this. I was already frightened of men, and acted very distant towards them. Never the less, one man in particular frequently followed me around in his van, offering me money to gratify him. I needed the money for food, so I agreed to do things to him, but I felt sick and disgusted by it. I never participated in the sexual act with any of these men.

Despite all the negative things in my life at this time, I still returned to the Lighthouse from time to time. I enjoyed the friendliness and kindness of the people, but now I was feeling frightened of God, and much further away from him. I thought that He could not possibly like me, let alone love me, because of all the bad things I had been doing. I started to feel so bad about myself that I took overdoses of painkillers on three or four occasions. I would go to a shop to buy the pills and a can of fizzy drink; then I would look for a quiet place to swallow the pills, a place where people were not likely to be watching me. Soon after taking the pills, I would become very fearful of dying; on each occasion I would then walk to the hospital, to the casualty department, where I would then have to have my stomach pumped out. This procedure was very unpleasant indeed, and I hated it. I would feel such shame and guilt for what I had done. They would put me on a ward, saying that a medical social worker would soon be coming to see me. The thought of this would put a massive fear into me, and I would then run out of the hospital, still wearing the hospital gown over my underwear. I would run like this all the way home. During this period in my life, I started bleeding again as a result of the earlier abuse that I had received. I received several operations over the space of the next few years to cure the problem, but these were not successful. This was mostly because I was allowed home too soon each time, and once at home, I was given jobs involving heavy lifting of coal or shopping, too soon after the surgery. The stitches would get broken and the surgery would then have been in vain.

CHAPTER 14

"Downward Spiral"

When the time came for my year group to sit their GCSE exams, I was taken aside and told that it would be a waste of Government money for me to be allowed to take any exams. Some of the other girls from our housing area were also told the same thing. Consequently, we all left school early that term, as there seemed to be no point in us hanging around. I didn't really understand the significance of all of this at the time, though it did strengthen the feelings of uselessness and shame that I already felt inside. I decided to try to look for some work. Earlier that year, I had been given the opportunity to help in a playgroup, for a few hours per day. I had really enjoyed working with the small children who attended there. The person in charge was an older lady, and she was a sincere Christian. She had been very kind and understanding to me while I was helping there. Even so, I didn't feel I could return to this work, as there would not be enough hours. Instead, I went to the "Young peoples' careers office", and they arranged for me to start a job at the local chicken factory. This job involved cutting up chickens into various portions, amongst other things. Needless to say, I hated it, and I only lasted three weeks in the job before I left. After this I stayed unemployed for a while, and would spend every day at the water meadows swimming and paddling with my dogs. Mum and Sally often came along too.

After the summer was over, I tried a few different jobs, all without success, until eventually I was offered a job as a checkout operator in a High Street supermarket. Surprisingly, I really liked this job, and after a while I was promoted to a checkout supervisor. My till was always balanced and correct, and with plenty of small change, which the manager liked to see. Unfortunately, Dad would often come into the store and create a scene. He would come to my till with a basket of provisions; then he would demand to have the items cheap or even for nothing. I would refuse, and he would create a fuss. Soon he was forbidden to come to my till, so the other staff would tell him to go to one of theirs. At this he would start to curse and swear, and throw some coins at them, telling them that they were robbing an old pensioner. After that he would start to walk out of the store and suddenly collapse on the floor. An ambulance would be called to take him to hospital. But, by the time I got home in the early evening, he was back home or down the pub, apparently fit and well. I found this behaviour of his extremely embarrassing and humiliating. Eventually, by the spring of the following year, it had become too much for me, so I decided to leave the job.

About this time, I went to an Indian restaurant for the first time, on my own. I ordered a meal from the English menu because I knew nothing about Indian food. One waiter in particular showed interest in me and acted kindly towards me. He told me that I didn't have to pay for my meal, and he asked to meet me the next day to go to the cinema. I was naïve enough not to see the dangers ahead of me, so I met this man the next day, but I did take Sally along with me. The Indian man, who I called Jimmy, kept to his word and took us both to see a film; afterwards Sally and I went home. I had agreed to meet him at a disco in another town nearby, a few days later. Once again, I took Sally with me. This time, Jimmy became angry with me. This was because Sally was too young to go in at only thirteen, and we had to go somewhere else. Over the coming weeks, Jimmy took the opportunity to introduce us to some of his friends. He paid for meals, and even bought clothes for us. Now he began to make sexual advances towards me, but I was very scared, so I pushed him away. Some of his friends also tried to make advances towards me, and one man became so angry with me that he threatened me with a carving knife from the restaurant kitchen. Jimmy managed to calm him down, for which I am very grateful, because the other man was ready to kill both Sally and me. I never went to that restaurant again, but I continued to meet Jimmy, because he treated us to things and promised to take me on holiday to India.

While all this was taking place, unexpectedly, my brother Johnny arrived home. This time it was supposed to be permanent, and not just a visit. As soon as he arrived, he announced to me that it was "pay-back time" for Dad. I felt shocked and frightened because I could see in his eyes that he meant it. There would be many curses and threats of violence to follow between them, causing Mum to end up in hospital again, as she couldn't cope with the atmosphere in the house. Meanwhile, Johnny started to tag along with Sally and me when we went out with Jimmy and his friends. Like us, Johnny also enjoyed receiving the free food and entertainment. Apparently, these Indian men were trying to get passports issued for the three of us, but none of us had birth certificates, as Mum had lost them. They told us that they wanted to send us on a holiday to India, but I realised later that they had other motives for sending us there. Motives to make money for themselves out of us. It would not have been a holiday, that's for sure, and we would probably never have returned.

After Johnny's return home, we also started to get into crimes involving "breaking and entering." This all started because we had no television or record player at home. We did have a television whilst I was working at the store, because I paid the monthly rental. But the television had been returned when I stopped working. We started to do burglaries at night, taking with us a pram to carry the stolen items, and both the dogs, (to give them a walk!) We burgled a college and a boarding school, both more than once. The first time, we took home with us a television set and record player, several packets of chocolate and cigarettes, and a petty cash tin. When we broke it open, it contained a small amount of cash. When we arrived home and carried in the television set, Dad looked up and said to Johnny

"Where did you get that?"

"It fell off the back of a lorry," Johnny replied.

Dad nodded and said nothing more. He was then happy to have it indoors, and to watch it. On at least one occasion, when we returned to the scene of a previous crime, we found the Police were already waiting there, as we could see a torch or a flashlight. We had to make our getaway through people's back gardens, with the pram and the dogs. We had to hide behind bushes and trees, and take a route home without going onto any main roads. We always managed to get home safely each time, and the Police did not come to our house. All this continued once a week or so over a period of about six weeks. I was feeling so bad and so evil during this period that I took overdoses on two occasions, and had to go to the hospital. I did talk to a psychiatrist both times, but because of guilt and fear, I could not admit to the real reason for the overdose.

One day, I was out with Sally and some other friends near the centre of the town, and we climbed on a wall near the back of the Indian restaurant. Sally and some of the others started to throw stones at the kitchens, which were at the back of the building. Someone inside must have called the Police, as suddenly two Policemen appeared with a ladder, and climbed up onto the wall close to where we were. We ran to escape across an asbestos roof, but Sally only made it half way across before the roof partially gave way. Sally's leg was trapped and bleeding, and she was screaming with the pain. The Policemen managed to rescue her and pulled her out; meanwhile the rest of us, under my direction, gave ourselves up. We were escorted down the ladder to a Police vehicle, and driven off to the Police Station. At the Station, we were all sitting in a room together, and Sally had her leg up on a desk so that her wound could be attended to. Meanwhile, a detective came in to collect something from the desk, and he stared at Sally's leg. She had a hole in her shoe, and he had been investigating the burglaries at the college. One of the footprints left behind had shown a shoe with a hole in it. The detective asked the policeman

"What are these kids in here for?"

"For being a public nuisance and throwing stones." the policeman replied.

The detective said; "I think they've been up to far worse that that! I'm taking over here."

Then he took Sally's shoes off her feet, and compared them to the prints they had found at the burglary. After that, he took details of our names and addresses and let us go home. But next morning the Police arrived early at our house and I was taken to the Station on my own for questioning. The detective was scary and aggressive, and I had to give him information of the places we had visited, who had been involved, and what had been stolen. He had already noticed some of the stolen items when he went to our house. Later, when he returned to our house to bring Johnny to the Station, he recovered the television and the record player. Dad had been sitting in his armchair watching T.V., when the detective came in and said to him,

"Do you realise that you have been watching stolen property all this time?"

Dad pointed at Johnny, and replied,

"But he told me that it had fallen off the back of a lorry!"

The detective smirked and said,

"You're lucky you're too old to be arrested and taken down to the Station, for aiding and abetting!"

Johnny joined me at the Station later in the morning and Sally came in at lunchtime from school, accompanied by a social worker, due to her age. Eventually, we were charged and released on bail by the evening. Mum had been brought in earlier, and she was getting herself in a terrible state, shouting loudly for her kids and threatening to walk out and throw herself under a car. The detective had become less aggressive to me now that he had information, and he was telling me to co-operate in Court, so things would go easier for us. Of course, I trusted nobody, so I took little notice of what he said. I was in a very nervous state by now, and was exhausted and shaking. Eventually we all were allowed home, and we had about eight weeks to wait for our Court hearings, though each of us had been given different dates and times to appear.

During this period of waiting, I was in an anxious state most of the time, and I had no money to buy food for the family and the dogs. I visited the Indian restaurants that I had known before, and this time I agreed to do sexual favours for money. Once I had done something for one of them, there were others wanting favours from me too. I was happy to get some money, but I hated what I had to do for it. However, at no point was I involved in actual sexual relations with any of them. In fact none of them even touched me; they seemed very remote from me emotionally, and I was totally detached from what I had to do for them.

By now, I was acting rather like a wild person, going wherever I wanted and doing whatever I felt like doing. I had no love in my life and little discipline either. After a few weeks had passed, I duly appeared in court for the first time. The hearing was very quick, though they included charges for other crimes with which we had not been involved. I was not given any opportunity to speak. I was remanded to a bail hostel in another town which was about thirty miles away, and I was due to appear again in three weeks time. I was taken away from Court by the social worker with the small car. We collected some belongings from home, and then I was driven to the hostel. It turned out to be run by Catholic nuns. While I was there, I took two further overdoses of pills. I spent most of the time wandering around the town, sometimes taking myself to the funfair, which was located nearby, and mostly just trying to survive. I was missing my home and my dogs very much. On three occasions, the nuns had to call a doctor to inject me with a sedative, because I was in such a state of anxiety and fear. I felt miserable inside, full of hopelessness and despair. There seemed little hope of anything getting better. Little point in even staying alive.

CHAPTER 15

"Hope and Despair"

The final week had come that I was due to spend in the bail hostel. I was having some supper, when one of the nuns announced to everybody there that a Christian meeting was due to take place at the Guildhall that very evening. She said that any of us were welcome to go along, if we were interested. Because of the Lighthouse meetings back home, I was interested in going; another girl was interested in going with me, even if mostly out of curiosity. We walked together to the Guildhall, and when we arrived, two men, who were standing at the door, welcomed us. We went in and sat by ourselves in the middle of the hall, at the end of a row. About five minutes later, the worship group came on and began to sing songs. The audience stood up, and began to sing and clap with their hands raised to the ceiling. I felt very frightened inside, and I couldn't cope with the atmosphere of joy and praise. Fear overwhelmed me, and I suddenly made a run for the nearest exit, dragging my new friend with me, against her wishes. We went straight back to the hostel, even though the other girl was trying to change my mind. I felt really bad inside, because I had escaped from the meeting, and I didn't understand why.

The next day I felt downhearted and despairing again, yet when the evening came, something inside was pushing me to go back to the Guildhall again. I asked the other girl from the hostel, but this time she refused, saying that I would only run out again. So I went back, this time on my own. To my surprise, the same two men at the door recognised me and invited me to come and sit with themselves and their wives. Although I didn't know them at all, I could tell that they were kind and sincere, so I found myself agreeing. I took my seat between one of these men and his wife. Again the music, singing and clapping began, and again I started to feel overwhelmed with fear, wanting to run out. But the couple managed to prevent me from leaving by saying,

"No, please don't go. This part of the evening won't last very long, and then a man will come and speak to us. We believe that you'll be very interested in what he has to say."

I was curious about this, and managed to stay there with them. Sure enough, after a little while, the music and singing came to an end, and a small dark-haired middle-aged man wearing a shiny suit, walked onto the stage. He began to speak with fiery passion, often quoting verses from the Bible. He told us that the end of this age on the Earth was drawing near, and that Jesus Christ was alive and had risen from the dead. He would soon be coming back to receive his followers, his Bride. I remember him saying that this might happen within the next fifty years or so. The man went on to say that anyone who did not have a personal relationship with Jesus, by asking Him to come into their hearts, would end up in Hell, like the devil. Of course there was much more that he said, and I had heard some of this before at the Lighthouse, but I had never responded to the call to repent and believe. Right now I felt very frightened at the thought of going to hell, even though I felt I deserved to go there. When he made an invitation for people to come to the front to receive salvation, I was out of my seat in a flash and was one of the first to reach the front to receive Jesus into my heart. I followed the words of the prayer that was given, and was taken out to another room with about fifty others who had responded. We were given a little talk and some literature. Meanwhile, the couple that had sat with me joined me and gave me their address and telephone number. They said they would like to take me to their church that Sunday evening. I followed up on this invitation by telephoning them a couple of times, and I did go to their church on Sunday. Here I received a welcome, which was almost overwhelming for me at that time. I also heard for the first time some people "praying in tongues", (like in Acts Chapter 2 of the Bible), but I thought they were a group of foreign people, rather rudely interrupting the prayers by talking in their own languages. Since I had accepted Jesus more out of fear than in love, I was still plagued with anxiety and despairing thoughts. However, one thing I did notice was that my swearing had suddenly stopped.

The following Monday morning, I was due back in Court. The social worker with the Mini arrived to collect me. As we drove along in his car, I told him all about the meeting that I had been to, and that I had become a Christian. To my disappointment, he seemed most unenthusiastic about it! We arrived at the Court, and the authorities were concerned about the overdoses I had taken and the sedatives I had been given. They decided that I was a great risk to myself, and should be hospitalised by means of a "Section Order." However, there were no beds available at any of the local psychiatric facilities, and the only available bed they could find was in the psychiatric wing of Holloway Women's Prison, in North London. They told me I would be there for three weeks, while they gathered further psychiatric reports.

I heard all their discussions, and when I saw the two policemen coming to take me away, I suddenly felt as if my whole world had just ended. I lunged forward, and made a dash towards the table where the probation officers were sitting. I tried to leap over the table, intending to try to jump right through the glass window, which was two storeys up. But somebody must have grabbed my leg, and after that I think I blacked out. The next thing I can remember was someone taking my photograph, and then being taken to the local police station. I had to wait in a cell, and during this time I took off my tights and tried to strangle myself. Four policemen came rushing in; they ripped my clothes off me and put me in some sort of gown. One of them then stayed there with me for my own protection. Not long afterwards, three other police officers arrived, one female and two male, and they took me to a special vehicle. I went with them on the long drive to Holloway, dressed once again in my ripped clothes. I felt like I was engulfed in blackness, as if I was being swallowed into a great pit of despair. Eventually we arrived in North London, and I was handed over to the prison officers, all of whom were women. I had to take my clothes off again and was now given prison clothes to wear. Then I was taken along many corridors and up many staircases until we reached the wing where I was to stay. At first, I was put into a cell with five other women. They swore and cursed a lot, and talked about their crimes. They kept abusing the name of Jesus, which now I didn't like. I was scared of them and didn't want to talk to them or be near them. Then a prison officer came and gave everyone medication. She gave me some blue medicine to drink down, which smelled like the sea. This had the effect of knocking me out for the night. The next morning, I was moved into a smaller cell for just two people. The prison routine was that you came out of your cell for three meals a day; however there would often be disruption, with two or more women starting a fight. This would mean that all the women were locked up again in their cells without finishing the meal. The offenders would be taken to the "strip-cells" to cool off. Apart from the meal times, the only other times we had out of our cells was for half an hour of exercise after lunch, and half an hour of relaxation in the evening. So I was locked up for a long time each day with another woman. We talked a bit about our lives, but I could tell that she was also not in a good mental state. Then, on the second day, we were talking together, when she suddenly flipped, and smashed the mirror with her bare hands, cutting her wrists on the glass. I tried my best to restrain her, and while I was doing that, several prison officers burst in, grabbed us both, and took us down to the "strip-cells." They put me in a bare cell with only a mattress in it. They took my prison clothes away and gave me a grey sleeveless gown to wear. There was no heating, pillow or blankets, so it felt very cold. I shivered all night. The next morning, they must have realised that I had not had anything to do with the incident, and someone apologised to me and gave me back my prison clothes. They took me to another cell, which I was to share with an elderly lady. Word was that she had committed a very serious crime many years ago, and had been in this prison for a long time. She had made herself at home here with her knitting, her cards and books, and she never seemed to leave her cell. This was possibly because she had become very arthritic. This lady accepted me into her cell and was kind to me. Perhaps this was because I was only due to stay for a couple more weeks. She even tried to teach me to knit, and we played cards together. I felt safe with her, particularly as many of the other prisoners were very disturbed and many displayed lesbian tendencies. I had already received several invitations during break times, with offers of chocolates or roll-up cigarettes, but I refused all these.

During the evening exercise periods over the next few days, I would pass a cleaning cupboard, which was located in a quiet corridor. I took this corridor to try to avoid the other inmates. I liked to stop and look out of the window at the sky, and think about home and my dog. One such evening, I was aware of a noise inside the cupboard, so I peeped round the door to see what it was. There I found a middle-aged Caribbean woman wearing a green overall; she was sorting out some cleaning equipment. She saw me standing there, smiled broadly and greeted me.

"Hello dear," she said, in a voice that sounded like warm chocolate. "I haven't seen you before. Tell me now, are you new here?"

She asked me what my name was. I told her. Then we talked together for about fifteen minutes. I found her very gentle and kind; not at all threatening to me. When it was time for me to go, she said,

"You are most welcome to come back and see me again, my dear, if you want to."

Reaching into her bag, she pulled out a bar of chocolate, and gave it to me. Over the following ten days, I saw her about three more times. She was not always there when I came looking, but when I did see her, we would talk about our families and where we lived. She would also tell me that I was a good person at heart, and that I didn't belong here in prison. Whenever I had to go, she would smile and give me a big motherly hug. I had never experienced affection like this before, and the memory of it has stayed with me. I was still quite sedated from the nightly blue medicine, which meant that I was more able to receive these hugs than if I had been in my usual state of agitation and fear. I now believe this dear woman had been placed there in that prison by God, to bring light and love to other women in that very dark place.

The day before my second Court appearance was due, I was very surprised when a prison officer came to my cell and told me that I had visitors. I didn't have any idea who they might be, and it was a long walk down to the visiting room. They had to unlock doors and lock them again behind, and we also went down various staircases. Eventually, we reached the visitors room, which was a big room with tables and chairs. It was filled with other prisoners talking loudly to their visitors. The prison officer took me to a table, where two women were sitting. One of these was a stranger to me, but I recognised the other one. Her name was Heather, and she and her husband Peter had been organisers at the Lighthouse, back in my hometown. They had not forgotten me from those days. They had now moved to a town in the West Country, but somebody from the Lighthouse had telephoned them saying that they had seen a report in one of the local newspapers about me. They had already been doing work behind the scenes via Social Services and Probation Services, to see whether it might be possible for me to be fostered by them for a period of time. Now they had come to ask me if I would agree to their speaking up for me in Court the following day with this proposal. Naturally, I was ready to jump at any offer of help, and when I told them that I had become a Christian while at the bail hostel, they were thrilled and delighted, and even more willing to help me. After their visit, I went back to my cell with my head spinning, wondering what would happen the next day. I had been let down many times before, so I didn't dare be too hopeful.

CHAPTER 16

"New Horizons"

I had to get up at five o'clock in the morning in order to be taken back to my hometown, where the Court hearing was due to take place. My own clothes had been returned to me, and I duly put them on, but they were still damaged and torn from the incident in the police station. I was driven in a police van the whole way, without making a stop. On our arrival, I was taken first to the police station, where I was offered something to eat and drink. Soon the time came for them to take me to the Court. My emotions felt dead, probably due to the blue medicine I had been given every night. I was escorted into the Courtroom from the back of the building, and I was taken to one particular seat. A short time later, three magistrates came in, but they only spoke to me to confirm my identity. They proceeded to read out all the charges against me once again. Then they received reports from a solicitor for the defence, whom I myself had never even met, as well as from Holloway Prison and the Probation Service. All these reports included various suggestions concerning my future sentencing, while the Prosecuting solicitor was proposing that I spend two years in "Borstal", which is a prison for younger offenders. At this stage of the proceedings, Peter, whose wife had visited me in Holloway, was called to the witness stand. He spoke for several minutes, explaining that he had known me since I was quite young, as well as my brothers and my sister, and that I had often attended his club for young people. He also stated that I had been very helpful to him in the past, by helping to look after his children at a time when his wife was in hospital. He explained that I had been forced to grow up in very difficult circumstances, and that I had got myself into some trouble. But, he stated, that in his opinion I was of good character, and needed to be given another chance in life. For this reason, he and his wife were offering to have me come to live with them in their own home. He further stated that they lived in another town, about sixty miles away, and far from the influences of my family. Here I could be encouraged to make a fresh start. When Peter had finished speaking, the prosecutor tried to put him off the idea, by asking,

"Do you have a television set in your home? And do you have a record player?"

"No, I don't," Peter answered.

"Well you had better go get one of each," replied the prosecutor with a smirk, "Otherwise you might wake up one morning to find them sitting in your living room."

A muffled sniggering noise went around the Courtroom. Peter also smiled, but then composed himself.

"Yes, I have already thought about this," he replied, "and I am ready to purchase these items later this afternoon, as soon as I return."

The prosecutor continued to make some other negative comments, hoping to make Peter change his mind about having me, but Peter stood firm. The magistrates then instructed Peter to return to his seat at the back of the room while they left to discuss their verdict. Eventually, they came back into the Courtroom, after what had seemed like at least half an hour. I was asked to stand up to receive the verdict. They had come to the decision to allow me to go to live with Peter and Heather for a minimum of two years, and during this time, I would not be allowed to return to live at my home address. In addition, I was also placed on probation for a period of five years and there were also some costs to be paid. I felt very happy and relieved to be free again, and I began to feel my emotions again. I left the Courtroom that day and travelled by car to the "West-Country" with Peter and Heather.

On the very first evening in their home, Heather took me to see a film starring Elvis Presley. This was helpful to settle me in. However, that night I could hardly sleep, as my body had got used to the blue medicine. On the second night, I became very restless; I went out at midnight into the street, and knocked on the door of Jean, a friend of theirs who lived up the road. I had only met her that same afternoon. Jean shared her house with a missionary lady by the name of Sister Pat, and both were unmarried. At first, they didn't open their front door, but Jean looked out from an upstairs window and seeing who it was, she then came down in her dressing gown, to open the door. Once inside, the two women could see that I was very agitated. Sister Pat, who was a trained nurse, said that I was suffering from withdrawal symptoms from medication, and I needed to see a doctor as soon as possible. Jean phoned Peter, who came and fetched me home. The next day, I was taken to a doctor, and I was given some medication. The doctor was horrified when I described the medicine I had been given in prison, and said that it could have been potentially dangerous to me. Over the course of a week or so, I calmed down inside and was able to sleep again.

Peter and Heather began to take me to their church, and to some Christian meetings in the local area. I began to meet some other Christians, including an elderly Pentecostal pastor and his wife. Even though their dwindling little congregation consisted only of elderly women, they took a great interest in me. I would turn up at their house without warning in the morning or the evening, and they would always welcome me and offer me something to eat. I would often play "Scrabble" with them, which helped me learn to spell better. They also had several records by a gospel band called "Living Sound," which I used to find comforting, healing and peaceful. The band were all Americans, but they had a base locally, as I would later find out. I also visited Jean and Pat sometimes at weekends, and they would talk about different things. Jean would let me have a banana to eat, something I had never tasted before! I would also see them at church on Sundays, and they sometimes took me to Christian meetings happening locally. We all went to hear a lady called Jean Darnell. I was very taken by what she said and how she prayed for people, and I also received some prayer from her. She seemed so joyful with a warm smile, and very confident in her faith and her relationship with Jesus. I was very drawn by this, and I wanted to become like her. A month or so later, I was taken to a meeting with a speaker called Trevor Dearing. I was even more impressed with what he said and did, especially when he prayed over the room, and a blanket of God's peace came down and rested over all the people. I had never felt peace like this before; it was like spending a few moments in Heaven. Again I thought how I would like to be like this speaker one day. Meanwhile, I was helping Heather at home with housework and taking her children out to the local parks. After about a month, a man from the local church we attended, who owned a hardware store, offered me a part-time job. I would go there from two till six in the afternoons, five days per week, and I did some cleaning, tea-making, and general duties around the shop. People were friendly, and I enjoyed working there; there was a nice atmosphere and I felt accepted. I was growing in my faith, and was starting to bloom.

I had not been aware that Peter and Heather were planning to sell their house, and after only three months with them, they suddenly announced that they were moving to a larger town about fifteen miles away. The move came very quickly, and I had to give up my job and leave the friends that I had made. The house was new, very different from their previous older-style house. We all started to attend a house-church nearby, and some people befriended me, though it was not the same as the previous church. I now had no job, so I wandered around the town a lot, as well as helping with housework for Heather. I even sneaked back on the bus to visit my old friends a couple of times, because I felt lonely.

One "high-spot" was going with Heather to a meeting with a speaker called Jackie Pullinger. She is well known for obeying God's call to Hong Kong, and for her work with drug addicts and the poor on the streets. I was very taken by what she was saying, but I became agitated by the sheer love glowing on her face. I found myself getting restless, moving my chair around noisily, and I had to be escorted out of the hall. But the woman, who escorted me out, stayed and talked with me until Jackie had finished speaking. Then I was taken up for prayer, along with a line of others. Jackie came straight over to me first, but she didn't pray. Instead she looked intently at me, and asked if I could be taken back to the place where she was staying that evening. It was agreed, and Heather came along with me. We left straight away, and were taken there in a car; but we had to wait a long time for Jackie to arrive after the meeting had finished. When she did come, she talked to me for a little while, and then started to pray for me; but she said there was a blockage "in the Spirit". I had to renounce and repent of some occult influences - reading horoscopes, doing palm reading, etc. Then I was amazed when she "picked up" that I had some stolen property. These were items that I had "borrowed" without permission. There was a leather jacket, which I was actually wearing and which wasn't mine, and a portable radio, which was back at the house. I had to repent and promise to return the items to their owner, which I did the next day. I learnt that borrowing without permission was really the same as stealing. Then she prayed again and I received the Holy Spirit. He came in waves, and I felt some joy and peace and I began to speak in tongues. I was given prophetic words via Jackie concerning my Mum, myself and some other family members, that I held the key for their salvation. She saw a picture of my family in great spiritual darkness, and myself with a key to unlock the light of salvation to them. Jackie warned me that all of this would only happen if I stayed walking with God. If I did not, my family would be doomed, without salvation. Afterwards, Jackie offered for me to correspond with her for my encouragement and help, which I have done from time to time since.

Meanwhile, Heather was wanting me to go to a Christian hostel in London, where I could receive training, but I felt quite threatened by this idea. Finally one day, she arranged everything for me to go, and I even caught a train to London with my suitcase packed. Jean had given me some money in an envelope, but when I arrived in London, I felt really lonely, and I used this money to buy a ticket for another train, going back to my old hometown. I arrived at the station, and took a taxi. It seemed very strange arriving home again, and I wondered what sort of reaction I would receive. I walked in, and Mum was there by herself. She was very surprised and pleased to see me; but Donny, my dog, was even more "over the moon!" He jumped at me with tail wagging furiously, and licked my face, all the time barking with great excitement. I was very happy to see my dog again. I told Mum that I was home again to stay. Amazingly, only six months had passed since the Court hearing, but I had been told to stay away from home for two years!

CHAPTER 17

"New special friends"

I quickly fell into my former way of living, trying to do housework and looking after Mum and our two dogs.

I did try to get a job, but I couldn't get one because of my prison record. I was still on probation, and I had been reporting to the probation service every week while I was staying with Peter and Heather. Although I was now supposed to be in London, I quickly reported to the local probation office, here in my hometown. On my first visit, I talked to the chief probation officer. It turned out that he was also a Christian. He agreed for me to stay at home for the time being, provided that I was actively looking for other accommodation. He assigned one of his probation officers to me. She was a kind person with a positive attitude towards me, and I took a liking to her. She has remained a friend up to this day. Unfortunately, the atmosphere at home was still bad, a lot of the time. Whenever Dad and Johnny were both at home, they would frequently threaten to kill one- another with a knife. It was usually Dad that started a fight, but Johnny would rise to the bait every time. Their shouting and swearing would often get so loud that neighbours would call the police, who would pull up outside our house in one or more police cars. Three or four policemen would come running down the stairs to the basement, where our living room was situated. The moment Dad saw the police running in, he would burst into tears and cry,

"Help me, help me; he's trying to kill me!"

Meanwhile Johnny, still full of hatred and rage, would turn his anger and abuse on the police. Then he would tell the police that it was Dad who was threatening to kill him, that they should arrest Dad, and take him away. Needless to say, the police always sided with the "help-less old man", and threatened to take Johnny down to the cells and into the "cooler." Only once did Johnny actu-ally get arrested. He and Dad had got into a fight over television programs, and in the heat of the argument, Johnny punched Dad hard. Dad came flying backwards, crashing straight into me, as I was coming in into the living room. I softened the impact, as Dad would other-wise have hit the wall. He might have been badly hurt. Even so, Dad had lost one or two teeth, and his mouth had started to bleed, causing blood to get on my clothing.

During this time of turmoil at home, I was looking for a "charismatic" church to attend, where I could be loved and nurtured. At first I went along to the local Anglican Church, which was on the edge of our estate. I found the services dull and boring, but the vicar himself was kind and caring, and wanted to try to help me. He took me in his car to various Christian centres in the county and beyond, trying to find accommodation for me, but noth-ing came of it. He realised that his church services were dull for someone like myself, and he suggested that I try a local "Pentecostal" church. I went along to this church on foot one Sunday, and the people there seemed quite friendly to me on my first couple of visits. However, over a period of one or two months, the leaders started to challenge whether I was a true "Born again" Christian. This was probably because of the way I looked and acted. They would say,

"You're not a Christian. You need to say the sinner's prayer."

They would quote a Bible verse over and over to me that said that "when a person is in Christ, they are a new creation, and old things are passed away." In their eyes, I didn't fit that description. Yet, I knew I was a Christian deep inside, so I refused to say this prayer just because they told me to. I felt anger and rejection inside, and I also felt that God was telling me not to give in, but to stand for what I believed. Eventually, one day, after three or four months of this treatment every Sunday, I became so upset and angry that I picked up a wooden chair and threw it across the church building. Then I ran out of the church, and didn't go back there for a year or more.

I returned to the local Anglican church for a short time, until the vicar told me that he had found a Christian holiday centre in Yorkshire, which had agreed to have me go to stay and work there. I didn't want to upset him, so I left the following day, feeling lonely and apprehensive, and I travelled on my own by train, all the way up to the Yorkshire dales. I was met off the train by a couple, and taken to a large house in the middle of nowhere. Immediately, I felt overwhelmed by feelings of loneliness and I felt very homesick. After a day or two, I found that I could talk to and mix with some of the guests, but I found the house-rules and all the chores too overwhelming. After a few days, I started to mingle even more with the guests, and one or two of them even took me with them on outings. One couple were very wise and helpful with what they said to me, but I was not yet ready to receive their advice. I was also able to join in with the meetings and games in the evenings. The people in charge of the house quickly realised that I was not ready to help and work in a place like this, and they told me gently that I should go back home. They kindly let me stay on for two weeks, during which time I was allowed to walk their dog for a couple of hours every day. Meanwhile, knowing that I was not supposed to be at home, rather than go back there, I telephoned Jean. She told me I was welcome to come and stay with her for a few weeks. She even sent me some money by post, so that I could buy the ticket. So, off I went again, back to the West Country, to the small town where I had first lived with Peter and Heather. When I arrived at the station, Pat was waiting for me. She took me in her car to their house, where I was given the little study as my bedroom. It was full of books, and I enjoyed reading some of these Christian books.

Needless to say, after a couple of days, I started to get bored. I was still a wild teenager, and they were older ladies with no television, and a strict routine. This included going to bed at nine p.m. I decided that I was going to go home again. I had previously met an old man during my time staying with Peter and Heather. This man, whose name was Joe, had been a prisoner of war, and I had been trying to convert him to Christ. Now I planned to try to persuade him to drive me all the way home. I went to his house just across the road, and asked him. He agreed to do it. However, I wanted to say goodbye to another friend before I left. This friend lived in a block of flats, and I got confused with the numbering. I finished up knocking on the wrong door. A man I didn't recognise answered the door, and he spoke with an American accent. For some reason he asked me in, and I accepted. Inside were three ladies and one other man, and all of them were Americans. I explained that I was looking for someone else and had rung the wrong bell. I told them where I had been staying, and that I was about to go back to my hometown. They then told me that they belonged to the gospel group called Living Sound, and that they were missionaries in England. One of the couples, Luther and Sandy, asked me if I would like to go on an errand with them to visit a nearby church. I agreed, not realising that it was actually an hour's drive away. When we arrived, Luther went in to discuss his business, while Sandy talked to me outside for a long time. We returned about mid-afternoon, and then I admitted to them that I was trying to run away back to my home. She lovingly helped me decide to change my mind. I had to go back to Joe's house to collect my suitcases, and he was angry with me for having been away so long. With Sandy's help, we got my suitcases back, and took them back to Jean's house. Thankfully Jean was still at work, and never knew about my plan to escape. However, Sandy stayed with me until Jean returned. She explained that she and Luther had met me today, and that they were willing to drive me to my hometown later that same week, because I had been summonsed to the court as a witness in a case between Dad and Johnny. So I stayed at Jean's house for a couple more nights; then the day arrived to travel to the Court-case.

Luther and Sandy collected me early in the morning, and drove me in a big American campervan. When we arrived at my hometown, we made our way to the court. After a short while, the court came into session. Dad, who was there as the defendant, was asked to swear on the Bible in the normal way. But every time he was asked to repeat the words, he couldn't say them properly, and after five minutes or so, the magistrate became exasperated with him and dismissed the case. Dad was led out of court doing his "Help me, I'm a helpless old man" routine. Somebody did take pity on him and paid for a taxi home, but he went to the pub instead. Meanwhile, Luther and Sandy took me to visit Mum at home. Mum was in a state about the case, and I was able to calm her down a little. Luther and Sandy didn't come in, but waited for me in their van, parked just around the corner. I didn't stay long in the house, and soon I was back in the van again. We talked a lot, and I shared some things about my past and my family. I liked this couple very much and felt that I could trust them, as they were kind and genuine with me.

After our return, I was given the chance to work in their offices for a few hours every weekday, writing envelopes for mail-outs. There were many hundreds to be done, and all of them by hand. I also folded up newsletters and items to be put into the envelopes, and stuck on the stamps. Sandy would explain to me what I had to do, and at the same time they would talk to me about the Christian faith, laying foundations. I was still quite wild and undisciplined, so they would try to teach me how to present myself in life. I enjoyed having the chance to be useful, and I felt accepted by them. It was helpful to receive teaching about living the Christian life, and I was never bored in the daytime. All this continued for about two months, as Jean had only agreed to have me stay for a few weeks. So, one day in November, I packed my suitcases, and said goodbye to all my friends, and travelled by coach back home. It was a bit of a shock to be back in that atmosphere, but I started to look after Mum and the two dogs again. I often felt lonely and depressed, but I spoke to Sandy every day by telephone. I would call from the payphone down the road, and she would always call straight back, no matter what she was doing. Without this, I would almost certainly have lost all faith and hope. I went back to visit Sandy and Luther immediately after Christmas, and I stayed three nights on a mattress on their living room floor. They gave me a Christmas present, a cuddly toy, and I was very touched by this. I had received presents at the children's home, but no one who was a friend had ever given me a Christmas present before. During the spring, Luther and Sandy came up to visit me at home, and they took me to a restaurant to buy me a meal. This was also a special experience for me. They walked either side of me, each holding my hand, and it gave me a sense of protection and security around me.

During the spring, my dog Donny, who had getting unwell for some time, became even more ill. He had received no injections as a puppy, as we had not been able to afford visits to the vet. I did manage to take him once to a free clinic in another town, where they had given him medication for a cough. But now, his hair was falling out and he had become very thin. I had started going occasionally to my previous church, and had been talking about Donny to a person there. They came to our house and saw the state of the two dogs and of the house itself, and asked if they could take both dogs for treatment without any of us accompanying.

"It will be better for you that way," the person said. Later that day, they returned without the two dogs.

"Both your dogs were in a terrible condition. Donny was suffering with cancer and various other ailments; Suzie had been allowed to have too many litters of pups, and was in poor condition. Your father is very fortunate that he is not being prosecuted for neglect and abuse of the dogs. The RSPCA have said that he is unfit to own another animal of any kind."

This person then left, without entering the house, having not told us what had happened to the two dogs, or where they had been taken. I was left feeling devastated, as if a part of me had been taken away. Over the following days, I found myself slipping into a dark hole; my dogs had meant so much to me. I spent days with feelings of depression, as if my best friend had been taken away from me. I also had feelings of guilt, because I felt that I should have done more for the dogs. I never did find out what happened to both dogs. Later that evening, Dad came back from the pub. "Suzie, where's my Suzie?" he was calling.

Mum told him that the dogs had gone.

"They've been taken away, and they're not coming back;" she said.

Before she had finished saying these words, Dad started to cry and call out;

"My Suzie. I want my Suzie!"

I was shocked by this outburst, as up to now Dad had showed little or no interest in the dogs, and would often swear and moan about them. After a few minutes, Dad stopped his outburst, and after that, never mentioned the dogs again. Then, a few weeks later, Dad came back from the pub carrying a kitten, which he named "Kibey", apparently after something connected with India. Dad had ignored the words spoken by the RSPCA officer.

CHAPTER 18

"Finding a new Church"

Meanwhile, I had to make a visit to the local hospital, where I was admitted for a couple of nights. I still hated hospitals, however one of the nurses was very kind to me, and she invited me to come and visit her at the nurse's accommodation once I was out of hospital. She was a Christian, and she attended an Anglican church in a different part of the town. Soon she introduced me to her friend Janine, who worked as a midwife at the hospital and also attended the same church. I hadn't been along to any church for a little while, so when they invited me to go with them, I accepted. I began to go along there regularly, and to my surprise, Mum decided that she would also come with me. It was a long walk from our house to this church, and Mum would get tired, and then often fall asleep during the sermon, snoring loudly. I found this rather embarrassing, but the congregation were too polite to say anything to us. They were mostly professional people and many were quite well off, so it was hard to feel well accepted. Never the less, I continued going to this church regularly, because I really wanted to be faithful to Jesus. After a while, Janine organised to take me to see two ladies in another town, who offered teaching and deliverance ministry. I have to admit that most of what they said to me went right over my head. Then they prayed over me some deliverance prayers, but I'm not sure exactly what God did. I was still quite wild and immature, and I was living in a house where there was still much darkness. My desperate longing was for peace, acceptance and love, but when at church I mostly felt and received the opposite. Looking back, I now realise I had a barrier of rejection and fear around me, rather like a thick castle wall, and I had body language to match. It was not surprising that most church people avoided me and didn't talk to me. Of course, I was not aware that I was sending out this message to others, so I just felt more hurt and rejected.

Thankfully, I was still speaking to dear Sandy every day by telephone, and in every conversation she would tell me that she loved me and that God loved me. At that time her words entered my ears and head, but never really penetrated into my heart. Never the less, they gave me hope, and I liked to hear them. About this time, and with a good word from my probation officer, I managed to get myself a part-time job at the Post Office, sorting mail. I enjoyed doing this job, and Dad could not pester me there, as he couldn't get access to the building. However, there was one man from my childhood who started to pester me again on a regular basis. This man would hang around outside the Post Office exit when it was my time to finish work. When I appeared, he would approach me, offering me money for favours. I kept telling him to go away. I told him,

"I am not doing those things anymore, especially as I am now a Christian."

But the man just laughed at me, and wouldn't stop pestering me. In the end, I got so fed up with it that I reported him to my probation officer. She was very wise. She told me to take a tape recorder with me, carefully hidden under my coat, and record whatever he said. Fortunately, I already had a portable battery operated tape player, which I used for listening to my Christian tapes. These included a tape by a singer called Len Magee. He had been rejected by his family in England and had ended up in a children's home in Australia, where he eventually became a Christian and eventually a Pastor. I felt that his background was very much like my own. So then, I armed myself with my tape player, and at the next opportunity, when the man started to pester me, I recorded his conversation with me outside the Post Office. After he had been pestering for a few minutes, I pulled the tape recorder out of my pocket and played it back to him. I also threatened to take it to the Police Station if he didn't leave me alone. He suddenly looked very angry and I feared that he might grab the recorder off me and even hurt me. But instead he walked away from me, swearing and muttering to himself, out loud. Thankfully this action worked, and this man did not try to pester me anymore.

At about this same time, a couple from the church offered to have me come and live with them for a while. I agreed, as I was still trying to find other accommodation away from home. This couple had been running an 18+ group at their house, and I had attended over several months, and enjoyed going there. The lady apparently had the belief that if I went to live with them for just a short time, my behaviour would change dramatically. At first, things went well. I shared meals with them, was allowed to do some cake baking and went on some outings with them. It was like being part of a new family, as they also had two young boys. I used to help with housework, as well doing my own washing and going to my part-time job. The lady also took me to visit another member of the church for a coffee. This was the first time that I had met this other person.

Meanwhile, I had to have yet another operation, but as before, it was not successful. For whatever reason, this turned me both emotionally and mentally unstable again. I started to have re-occurring stomach problems, being sick regularly, and I also had difficulties in sleeping. One morning, after I had scarcely slept all night, there followed a misunderstanding and upset with the lady of the house, during which I became very agitated and upset. I picked up a pair of sewing scissors in a threatening way, though I really had no intention of using them to harm anyone. However, the lady took this as a genuine threat to her life. She called for a doctor, and when he arrived, he decided to send me under a "section order" to a mental hospital. This was the same hospital that Mum had often visited as a patient. I was feeling very frightened and distressed when I arrived there, and they had to sedate me with an injection. When I woke up next morning I tried to stand up, but instead, I just collapsed onto the floor. I succeeded in getting up again, and this time managed to walk very unsteadily to the breakfast room. In my heart, I cried out to Jesus to come and be with me and to help me; I felt very frightened. To my surprise, I felt His peace come into me, and I was able to spend the next five days doing cross-stitching, and other gentle activities. After much questioning by the medical staff, I was allowed to go home. They had decided that I was not a danger to society. My probation officer came to collect me, and she took me in her car back to Mum and Dad's house.

Before long, I started to feel depressed, with a feeling of blackness around me. Wanting to make amends, I tried to go back to the family I had been living with, to try to talk to them. However, the lady was very threatened by see me, and refused to open the front door to me. I felt even more rejected by this because I thought they were my friends. In my mind, I didn't understand why they wouldn't speak to me. I became more and more upset and I started to shout

"I want to talk to you. Let me in!"

I banged hard on the front door, and suddenly the big pane of glass in the door broke, sending pieces of glass all over the place. I just stood there feeling dazed and upset, until a few minutes later, a police car pulled up. Two policemen got out and quickly took hold of me and put handcuffs on my wrists; then they took me to the police station. When I arrived there they talked to me; they didn't put me in a cell but they charged me with criminal damage to property. They issued me with a date for a Court hearing, and released me. I hurried straight to my job at the Post Office, because I was already late for work. Somehow I managed to do my shift and then went home. The next day was a Saturday. I was feeling frightened, and depressed, and was wondering what would happen to me. I thought I might have to go back to prison as I had broken my probation. I didn't know who to talk to, but I remembered the lady who had given me a coffee whose name was Hazel. I looked up her number in the telephone book. Then I called her from a phone box. I managed to talk to her by phone, and to my surprise, she invited me to come round to her house. I walked all the way to the edge of town where she lived, and I found that her husband, Frank, and her two children were also there. I spent the afternoon with Hazel and talked about what had happened. She listened to me carefully, and meanwhile a record about Joseph and his multicoloured dream-coat was playing. I found the music comforting and soothing. Later on, Hazel took me home in the family car. After this, I started to see Hazel once a week. She owned a small motorcycle, and I would ride on the back wearing her spare helmet. At her house, we would sometimes do some sewing, and sometimes some cooking. We would talk together while we were doing these activities. The day for the Court hearing was fast approaching. My probation officer had remained helpful and supportive after the incident, and she had suggested a good solicitor in the town. He was very kind and helpful towards me. When the day came for the hearing, Hazel attended personally to speak for me, and a letter had been received from the offices of Living Sound, giving a further positive appraisal of my character. Also, my probation officer gave a good report and my solicitor spoke well on my behalf. I did not have to speak at all during the hearing. At the end of the hearing, to my relief, the magistrates ruled that I was to pay the costs of any damage, and that I was to serve an extra year on probation. Sadly, a few days later, the Manager at the Post Office called me in and said that they could no longer employ me because I had been called to Court. I was very upset to lose my job, but a few days later, my solicitor turned up unexpectedly at home, with his wife. They asked if I would like to come and clean their house and do general household duties, three afternoons per week. I was very surprised, but I accepted. I worked for this couple for a few months, until Dad started to become very unwell, and I had to leave my work to help care for him.

CHAPTER 19

"Preparing the Ground"

As the autumn months passed, Dad was deteriorating physically. Two or three times, I had to go to the phone box down the road, to call a doctor. Dad would be holding his side, moaning in pain. On each occasion, the doctor came to our house and gave Dad some pills to take. This doctor came originally from Germany; he still talked with quite a strong accent.

"You know he's kicking the bucket?" he said to me, more than once. Unfortunately, I had no idea what that phrase about a bucket meant, so I would just smile and nod back. After that, he would just say, "Bye-bye," and leave in his car. Dad thought he had a hernia, so Mum thought the same; I thought he might be suffering from liver damage caused by too much drinking of alcohol.

In late October, Mum, Sally and I went along to the "Harvest Supper" evening at our new church. We arrived a little late, but as I walked into the church hall, I could hear music. I saw two men on the little stage, playing guitars, and singing. They were brothers, and the older one was leading with a song that he had written. The words told that we were like a radio, and we should let God tune us. As I watched and listened, a very unexpected thing happened to me. I suddenly felt as if I had known this man all my life. It was as if we were joined together in spirit; I part of him and he part of me. This feeling lasted less than a minute; then everything returned to normal. This was a kind of prophetic experience from the Holy Spirit, because at the time, this man and myself had never even met or spoken. Later on, however, this man was to become my husband.

Dad was still getting worse, and I had to call for the doctor again. This time, he came to the house, and called for an ambulance. I went with Dad to the hospital. He was taken into a cubicle, while I stayed outside. The hospital doctor tried to examine Dad, who then started screaming in agony. They decided to admit Dad into hospital for a blood transfusion, so I had to walk home on my own. The family still had not grasped how ill Dad was, yet we were surprised when, about two days later, Dad unexpectedly walked in through our front door, and he was looking a lot better. Apparently the new blood from the transfusion had given him a fresh lease of life, but this only lasted about a month. By the time we reached Christmas, Dad was poorly again; he had collapsed on several occasions on his way back from the pub. But still no one in our family or at the pub took it seriously. Everyone thought he had simply been drinking too much. But by mid January, Dad had stopped drinking altogether, even when we fetched a bottle for him to his armchair. He would try to drink, but he couldn't manage to. He had become very thin, both in face and body, and I had noticed blood on his trousers, as he dragged himself slowly up the stairs to bed. Then one day, near the end of January, he had been in the toilet for a very long time. I heard a thud, and running to the porch, I found him lying across the floor in a pool of blood, with the toilet door wide open. I heard him whisper in a weak voice

"Help me!"

I felt very frightened. I did not dare to touch him. Instead, I called Mum. Then I ran to the nearby phone box and phoned for the doctor. He came within minutes. By this time, Dad had managed to get back to his armchair. The doctor looked carefully at him and said

"I'm going to admit you to St Paul's Hospital."

Dad replied weakly; "No, I don't want to go there. My Dad died there."

The doctor replied; "Well then George, do you want your daughter to find you dead somewhere in this house? If you don't go to the hospital, that is what is going to happen, and it won't be a pretty sight!"

After those strong words, Dad reluctantly agreed to go to that hospital. Both Mum and I went with him in the ambulance. He went in great fear. Dad was admitted onto a ward, and I asked one of the doctors what exactly was wrong with Dad. This doctor replied; "Have you not arranged for the funeral? When he was in the general hospital, they diagnosed inoperable cancer and he was given three months to live. This disease had been left far too long before it was treated. He has less than three weeks to live."

I was very shocked by these blunt words. My thought now was,

"I've got to get him saved into God's Kingdom, because, at the moment, he's going to Hell."

I had to tell Mum what the doctor at St Paul's had said to me on the way home. She flipped straight into breakdown mode, saying it was too much for her and she couldn't cope. Next day I had to phone the doctor, and she was taken off to mental hospital again. So it was left to me to look after Johnny and Sally and visit Dad every day. And as if that wasn't enough, suddenly, in the middle of this stressful week, a social worker arrived, bringing Richard and Jeffrey back home, so that they could be there at their Dad's death. This gave me extra work and anxiety to cope with; neither of the boys seemed to be able to take any real interest in what was happening. Instead, they ran riot at the hospital, annoying both the elderly patients, and the nursing staff.

Thankfully, I was still managing to speak to Sandy every day by phone, and I would ask for prayer and support. On Sunday, I went on my own to church, and after the service I approached anyone I dared, asking for prayer for my Dad who was dying. One of the people I approached was the man who had been singing at the Harvest Supper. He seemed surprised and concerned by my approach, and he agreed to pray for my Dad, even though he had never met him. On Monday evening, Dad slipped into a coma. Hazel came to our house at about teatime to tell us, having herself received a call from the hospital. We all went up to the hospital that evening, staying until about ten o'clock in the evening. The following morning, we got up early. Johnny was now working for the Council, so he went off to his job. Meanwhile, I hurried up to the hospital, taking Sally, Richard and Jeffrey along with me. I had been told by Sandy to try to pray as much as possible in tongues, (in the Spirit), and to try to share the gospel with Dad, even if he seemed like he could not hear anything. I was very scared to touch him, or even speak to him, in case he suddenly woke up and swore at me. His last words to me before he went into a coma had been,

"Stop fussing, and "f" off; and leave me alone!"

I wanted to rescue him from Hell, so I prayed nearly all day. During the morning, the doctor and the hospital chaplain both visited together. The chaplain said the last rites over Dad, even though he was in a coma, and then they turned to me and told me that they expected him to die that day. After they left the ward, I continued to pray to God, and suddenly I had a vision. In the vision, I saw Dad lying dead; but his eyes were open and were bright blue, to match the blue sky outside. He looked younger and at peace, in a way that I had never seen him. I took this as a confirmation that God was going to take him to Heaven in answer to my faith. This encouraged me to continue to pray over him and speak words about God to him. Later in the afternoon, as his condition became worse and worse, I started to tell him to ask Jesus to forgive his sins, and accept Jesus as his Lord and Saviour. I had my hand over his hand; I plucked up courage and said to him;

"If you can hear me, wiggle your finger."

To my amazement, his middle finger moved back and forth under my hand. Then I asked him

"Have you received Jesus, and do you now believe in him?" To my delight, he moved his finger about again.

All this time, Richard and Jeffrey had been up to various pranks in the hospital. They were too young to be able to cope with something like this. Sally, tried to help, and had prayed with me at times. She had also tried to talk to Dad. By late afternoon, I asked her to take the boys to a nearby park, and they were gone for a long time. Meanwhile, Johnny arrived, having come straight from his work. He stood at the bottom of the bed, just staring at Dad; but he did not say a word. After a short time, Dad let out some horrible sounds. I was very scared, and called for a nurse to come. She came over quickly, but just said,

"Don't be afraid, that's called the death rattle. He is just passing on. It will be over soon."

Just as she said, within five minutes Dad had breathed his last breath. He looked nothing like he did in my vision. His face and eyes were yellow and sunken; and outside it was already dark. But I didn't let this put me off. I was offered a cup of tea, then Sally returned with the other two, to learn that Dad had passed away. Someone from the church came and kindly drove us all home, all except for Johnny.

Johnny went off by himself. The next I heard about him was when the Police called at our house in the early hours of the next morning.

"Johnny is in the accident and emergency department of the main hospital," the policeman reported.

Apparently he had got himself very drunk, and had knocked himself out by tripping over the pavement. Johnny had been shouting insults outside the police station, but they didn't press charges, after they learned that his Dad had just died. Johnny came home about five in the morning with a big bump on his head. He wanted to talk about Dad, about cancer and death. He was very shaken by what had happened, and just wanted to talk to me for about three hours. I was very tired and drained, but I managed to sit and listen to Johnny; I tried to give him some advice. That morning, I had to attend to all sorts of things. The first thing was to walk to the hospital to collect a death certificate so that I could register Dad's death and receive a certificate for burial. After this, I had to walk to the other end of town to visit the funeral directors. The man in charge was very kind to me. He seemed rather shocked that a person of my age was trying to do all these things on my own.

"Where is your mother?" he asked. "Why is she not doing this?"

I explained that she was in mental hospital. Then I had to explain that we had no money to pay for a funeral. The man referred me to Social Security for some help, and offered to bury Dad for free in the same grave where Dad's father was laid. I learned a little later that the vicar of my church had offered to conduct the proceedings without charge.

Unexpectedly, that same afternoon, Mum arrived at home accompanied by a social worker. She wanted to see Dad's body, in order to say goodbye. The social worker took us both up to the hospital, as his body was still there. Mum was very quiet. She just kissed him on the forehead, and was ready to leave again. But I was amazed when I saw him lying there. Outside it was a clear February day, with blue sky and bright sunshine. Dad was lying there with his eyes open, and they were clear blue, like the sky. His face looked white, but very peaceful, and with no lines on it. All this was exactly as I had seen it in the vision before his death, and it gave me great encouragement and comfort.

I visited the army barracks the following day, and they agreed to give Dad a military burial with a "union jack" flag draped over his coffin. The funeral took place about a week after his death. Sadly, no friends or relatives of Dad were present, but thankfully, a few people from the church congregation did come, as a support to our family.

CHAPTER 20

"Getting to know you"

After the funeral, the atmosphere at home was much better. It literally felt as if a weight had been removed, as there was no longer any swearing and fighting. Mum seemed very quiet, but showed no obvious signs of grieving. Johnny was still living at home, and he was able to continue in his job. Johnny was often out in the evenings, and liked to go to pubs, but he seemed calmer without Dad in the house. Richard and Jeffrey had been returned to their children's home the day after the funeral, but Sally stayed at home and she was now attending a local college. As for me, I had no job, but I did help Mum with things around the house. Mum was not receiving any money, because she and Dad had never married. His army pension had stopped with his death, so I made visits to the local "Benefits" office on her behalf, trying my best to get her some money to live on. After about a month, she did start to receive a small income, though it didn't go very far. Fortunately, one or two people from the church knew about our situation, and came by our house with groceries. One of these was the man whom I had seen playing his guitar, and who had agreed to pray for Dad on the Sunday before he died. This man's name was Bruce. He arrived with some bags of provisions and he stayed at our house for a little while, talking to Mum, Johnny and I. Over the following few months, Bruce took our family for some outings, mostly to try to cheer up Mum.

Johnny had now found himself a girlfriend, but she already had a young baby. Johnny invited her to move in to the house with her baby, without even asking us. I finished up looking after her baby, as she had no idea what to do. All this caused additional work and stress in the house. Then Johnny was involved in a serious incident in the town, which included being in possession of a dangerous weapon. Johnny was arrested and charged. He had to appear in Court later, where he was found guilty of an offence, and was sentenced to one year in borstal. [This means a prison for younger offenders]. The borstal was situated a long way from our home, about sixty miles each way. Bruce took us in a minibus to visit Johnny on more than one occasion.

Just after Johnny had been taken off to borstal, Richard arrived home from the children's home; he had recently turned sixteen. Richard was accustomed to a children's home environment, so he hung around aimlessly watching T.V. all day long, annoying the cat, and making no effort to find himself a job.

However, that summer, an opportunity came up for us all to go to France. This was organised by a charity, specialising in help for poor families. So off we went; Mum and I; Sally; Richard, and Jeffrey, who was allowed out from his children's home to join our family for the trip. There were also several other similar families travelling together with us first by boat and then by train. There were a few "helpers" who came along too, and these included Bruce and his friend Jimmy, who had both volunteered to accompany us. There were some good moments on this trip, but plenty of stress too; I was relieved to get back home after a few days away.

Only a month or so later, I was offered another holiday, this time by the probation service. It was a week in the Isle of Wight, and I was allowed to take Mum, Sally and Richard with me. We were to stay in a probation hostel in Newport, in the centre of the island, but we had to do our own self-catering. When the day came, my probation officer took us to the ferry. Another probation officer collected us on the island, and took us to the hostel. All went well until, the next day, Johnny's girlfriend and baby, showed up at the hostel, begging to be let in. They were not supposed to be there, and we didn't know how they had reached the island. Not knowing what else to do, we had to let her come in with the baby. Of course, we had to rearrange the sleeping accommodation.

The next day was a Sunday. Sally and I decided to visit a Pentecostal church we had noticed nearby, for their evening service. The atmosphere and the people were very friendly, and the service was very lively. After the service, I spoke to the Pastor for a long time. He asked me many questions about the family. Who we were? Where we were from? And where we were staying? He seemed very interested as I told him a bit about my background. Eventually, he offered to drive us back to the hostel, giving me a phone number to call him if we needed any help. He also gave me his name, which, to my amazement, I discovered was Pastor Magee. Yes, he was Len Magee, the man whose story I had read about a few years before.

By Wednesday of that week, Mum had sunk rapidly into a state of mental illness. This was largely due to the presence of the small baby. Mum had tried to do the baby's washing, when she did not have to. She had also begun to call out for Dad, and she was imagining being buried with him. All this scared and alarmed me, so I decided to try to call Pastor Magee. I found the number he had given me and made a phone call from a public telephone box. Pastor Magee answered my call himself, and came round immediately to assess the situation. He felt, as I did, that Mum needed to go immediately to the local hospital. He kindly took Mum and I in his car to the hospital, where they sedated and admitted her. Then she was quickly placed under a section order, ready for transfer to the mental hospital on the mainland. I was shocked, but relieved that Mum was being taken care of. I was also very grateful to Pastor Magee. Now I just wanted to go back home, so I gathered the rest of the family, including the mother and baby, and we caught the first available ferry the next morning. I had called Bruce the previous evening, from the hospital, and he came to collect us all from the ferry. Bruce took us home, where I soon discovered that our cat, Kibey, had gone missing. We looked all over, but could not find him. Sadly, he was never seen again. A few days later, a church member came to our house and took Johnny's girlfriend and her baby away to a "Mother and Baby" hostel in another town. Her departure was a great help to me, as I now had to look after things at home for several weeks, 'til Mum came back from hospital.

I had full responsibility for the house and family. I tried to clean and decorate the house, but it was a losing battle; things were too far-gone. Eventually, I went to the Council, to try to arrange a "swap" for a smaller Council house. They agreed to this, and within just a few weeks, we were moving to a slightly newer house, a short distance away. I had no job at this time. It would have been difficult to cope with a job as well as everything else. I was still attending church with Sally, but I struggled to feel accepted. I was still speaking to Sandy nearly every day by telephone, and I used to see Hazel once a week for cooking or sewing. I also used to phone Bruce, especially when I was feeling low, and I would quite often walk to his house. Usually, Sally would follow me around, wherever I went. Bruce shared his house with another man called Jimmy. Both of them had come to France with us. The four of us would talk or watch television, and we would also look at the Bible, and pray together. This was helpful to us all, and God would often give us little words of encouragement. At the back of my mind I still recalled the unusual experience that I had when I first saw Bruce, playing his guitar and singing in the church hall. I wondered what it meant, but I was still very afraid of men, probably because of my early experiences. Then, Bruce explained to me as gently as he could, about himself and Jimmy. They had been living together for about three years as a "gay" couple, when one Sunday they had gone along to a church, the one I was attending, responding to a need for peace within. After a few weeks had passed, both men had invited Jesus into their lives on the same day, and had become Christians. Now they still shared the same house, but no longer shared the same bedroom together. I felt quite surprised, but somehow not shocked or angry. In some ways I now felt much safer being around two men who were not likely to be abusive to me. Also, my faith in God was strong, even though my emotions were very disturbed. I believed that nothing was impossible with God, and if Bruce and I were meant to be together, then God would work it out. So the four of us continued to spend time together, and learnt to face difficult situations. It was a time for building trust and friendship.

Shortly after, I had to go to hospital once again for another attempt at fixing the problem I had experienced for many years. I hated hospitals and was full of fear, and after the procedure I couldn't settle or rest. I was agitated and kept wandering about, causing problems for the nurses. I felt like a trapped animal, and in the end, had to be given sedatives to force me to rest. Bruce came to visit me; he found a frightened and sedated person in a bed, wanting to escape.

I left hospital the following day; the fear left once I was out of the hospital building. A church member kindly organised for me to be taken to the homes of four or five different church families, in order to receive salt baths twice a day. I managed to avoid any heavy lifting during this time, and after a month or so, the doctor gladly pronounced that the operation had been a success. [Without this successful operation, I might not have been able to give birth to a baby in the future.]

A few days before Christmas, the time came for us to move house. Mum had now returned from hospital, and seemed much better again. She was glad to get out of that dark and dirty old house. Bruce arrived with an open topped van from his workplace, and Jimmy also came to help. Someone in the church, who owned a carpet shop, had brought some off-cuts of carpet. The day before the move, he and Bruce had fitted them in the new house. I had also cleaned the kitchen and bathroom, so we were able to move in the furniture and appliances in one go. The new house had three bedrooms. Johnny and Richard shared the biggest room; Sally and I had the middle-sized room, and Mum had to take the smallest bedroom with just a single bed in it. Downstairs, we had a living room, a kitchen and a downstairs bathroom. There was a tiny front garden, and a small area of grass to the rear. Soon, this house became home, and a few days later, it was Christmas. This year Christmas came and went without the kind of traumas we usually experienced as a family. Soon the days passed into another New Year; one that would hold new challenges for me.

CHAPTER 21

"Engaged and Married"

By now, Bruce and I were seeing each other quite regularly. Sally and Jimmy would often be present, but sometimes we would meet up without them. Apart from the outings, which usually included other members of my family, we tried to find time to be on our own. We were unable to act towards each other in a romantic way, but we liked to pray and seek God together. One evening, Bruce was taking me home after spending some time at his house. We were praying together in Bruce's car, which he had parked in a quiet spot. As we prayed, I received a very strong impression that God was asking us to take a big step of faith together. To get engaged! I was nervous about saying anything to Bruce, but the feeling grew stronger, so I spoke it out. For a few moments, Bruce was silent. He was greatly taken by surprise. This would be a very big step for him because of his past, from which he was largely unhealed. It would also be a very big step for me because of all my past experiences. We prayed together some more, trying to seek God's confirmation. Then after a few moments of further thought, Bruce spoke.

"O.K., let's do it! We'll go into town tomorrow and buy an engagement ring."

I know this doesn't sound very romantic, but we were stepping into new ground with God. This was more in the way of faith and obedience than courtship and love.

The next day was a Saturday. We had previously arranged, earlier that week, to pay a visit to an elderly Pentecostal man at his home, in order to pray for him. This man had been quite ill for several months, and we had previously visited him in hospital to pray for him. By now, he had become very frail and weak. We came to his home, and sat down with him, and Bruce prayed over him with laying-on of hands, asking God for peace and healing. Then to our great surprise, as Bruce finished praying, the old man began to speak in a loud voice. At first we wondered what was happening, then we realised that the words coming from his lips were a prophetic confirmation from God about our future together and His plans for us as husband and wife. God was saying that we would encounter much opposition, yet we would grow in strength from one another. There were also words that described the sort of ministry that we would be called to do together. To us, this was an amazing confirmation of our decision, taken the previous evening, giving us hope, encouragement and peace. This elderly man knew nothing about our decision to get engaged the night before, as we had told nobody. [Sadly, he passed away shortly afterwards, and never lived to see our wedding day.] We left his house that day, and went rejoicing into the town to look for a ring. Soon we were in a jewellers shop, and I tried on some rings. We couldn't afford anything expensive, but I soon found a ring that I liked. I had never worn a ring in my life!

Now we had to break our news. Bruce had to tell his friend Jimmy, who found the news difficult to receive to start with. However, by this time Jimmy had made a friendship with a girl at his work. In time, they also became engaged, and later married. I told my family members, who seemed to be generally happy about it. However, it was more difficult for Bruce to tell his family. Some had accepted Bruce's former lifestyle, and had not been enthusiastic about his turning to Christianity. Bruce's father did not approve of me, or of my background; he was very suspicious of my motives towards Bruce. Sadly, a similar attitude existed in the church, which we attended. Some people were positive about us, believing that our engagement was part of God's plan, but others were very suspicious or even antagonistic. This was very hurtful for me, but we pushed through the opposition, as we both believed that we were following God's leading.

During the next few months, Bruce was still employed with the family business, and I was living at home looking after Mum. By now, we had fixed a date for the wedding, which was to be 26th March in the following year. By then, I would be nearly twenty-three years old. Mum had no money for the wedding arrangements. [In actual fact, she had no idea that the bride's mother was supposed to be responsible for anything to do with the wedding!] So, Bruce and I were free to make all the arrangements our selves, which was both a challenge and a blessing. We experienced the favour of God over us as we made preparations. A neighbour living just across the road, offered to lend me a wedding dress. It was a beautiful dress, which she had worn at her own wedding over twenty years before. My friend Hazel, whose daughter was one of our bridesmaids, chose material with me, and made by hand the two bridesmaid's dresses. Another lady in our home group, a retired cookery teacher, made us a lovely three-tier iced wedding cake. The Vicar, who had grown very fond of us, offered us the church and choir for the wedding service without the usual charge. Finally, and our dear friends Sandy and Luther came down to help us on the wedding day itself.

When the morning of our wedding arrived, I felt quite nervous, yet I was at peace deep inside. Sandy came over to Frank and Hazel's house, and helped me to get ready. She did my hair and my make-up for me, and also helped arrange the dress. Then, she went to collect Mum and Sally, to bring them to the church. Meanwhile, we had asked Luther to be our "Best Man," so he was already with Bruce. Johnny, my oldest brother, had agreed to "give me away", as Dad was not alive anymore. He looked smart wearing one of Bruce's office suits. Richard and Jeffrey, also dressed in suits, made their way to the church from Bruce's house.

Now the time had come for me to make my appearance. I arrived at the church in Frank's car. I had to wait outside the church doors for a short while, with a very nervous- looking Johnny by my side, and two young bridesmaids behind me, wearing their pretty dresses. I heard the organ start to play the wedding march; we moved slowly forward up the aisle to the front, where Luther and Bruce were already standing. The service was very blessed. Bruce and I both felt the presence of the Holy Spirit giving joy and peace. The Vicar himself was very warm and smiling towards us, preaching a lovely sermon about Jesus at the wedding in Cana, turning water into wine. We sang three of our favourite hymns, and Sandy sang two songs beautifully. Another couple from the church also sang some uplifting songs during the signing of the registry. After the service had finished, Bruce's brother took all the wedding photographs, and the guests joined us for a buffet meal in the church hall. Bruce's father, who had previously acted in a negative way towards us, was gracious to us on our wedding day, kindly providing the champagne to drink.

After the reception, we left the church to drive to a hotel in the West Country. We only spent one night away, but for us, our honeymoon night was rather difficult. The next day, we travelled back home to prepare for our proper honeymoon abroad. We had decided to join a group travelling on a Holy land tour of Israel. This was the furthest that I had ever been away from home, and I was very nervous about travelling on a plane, but the journey went fine. However, when we arrived in Israel, I became very scared and homesick. I wanted to go back home! I became very uneasy and felt threatened by the men and boys, begging and following us in the streets. Our guide was telling us to be careful in the streets, and not to separate from each other, which only reinforced my fears. I managed to stay, and Bruce and I spent some time in the garden in Jerusalem where Jesus' tomb is reputed to be. We would sense a peace and presence there. We also went with the group to Galilee, and we saw many of the biblical sights and places. It was rather a hectic schedule for a honeymoon, but we didn't go on all the planned excursions. It was still a trip of a lifetime for us. On our return, we found Mum in a state of anxiety, because Sally had gone away from home, and had taken some possessions from the house with her. Sally had been seeing a man from another, with a troubled family background. Some people had advised her not to get involved with this man, but after our wedding, she went off with him to a town in the North of England. Three months after our honeymoon, I found out that I was expecting a baby. I felt very frightened because Dad had spoken words over me, saying that I would die in childbirth. This prevented me from feeling positive emotions. I received prayer from the vicar and his wife, and gradually I became less fearful. Meanwhile, Bruce prayed for the unborn child every day, and God gave us a boy's name and a girl's name, but we didn't know which would come first.

Also at this time, I received the fulfilment of the promise God had given me through Jacky Pullinger, a few years earlier. He had told me that if I continued to walk with him, and did not turn away, then he would bring my Mum into his kingdom. One afternoon, Mum and Richard were visiting our house. Bruce and I felt led to read a passage in the Bible to them from John's gospel, chapter one. Afterwards we asked if either of them would like to receive Jesus into their hearts, and Mum nodded that she would. So, we had the joy and privilege of leading her through the prayer to ask Jesus into her life.

As the months went by, Bruce was starting to become unwell. He would feel tired and drained, and would often come home from work to try to rest. However, this resting seemed to be of no help, and as winter approached, his health was getting worse. I was doing better, and I was starting to prepare for the baby, due in mid-January. I even tried to learn to drive a car that autumn, but I was running out of time, and had to give up just before Christmas. When Christmas arrived, we were about to receive a big shock. We attended Christmas Day lunch with members of Bruce's family, but Bruce's father seemed to be looking at us in a strange way. Two days later, after Boxing Day, Bruce received a phone call from his father, asking him to come and visit. On his arrival, Bruce was ushered into their dining room to be told that he was dismissed from the family business and removed from his father's will. Bruce was, however, permitted to keep possession of his company car as if it were his own. Bruce was now unemployed, and would have to "sign on" at the job centre for benefits. This news came as a great blow to us both, especially as I was only three weeks away from giving birth. Bruce, already struggling with his health, now felt useless and despairing. He had always felt unable to please his father, and this was now reinforced. His brother was angry and upset at the news, but had no power to do anything about it. As for me, I felt that everything was my fault, and that this had happened because Bruce's father didn't like me. We did have some Christian friends come and pray for us, and they too were surprised and shocked by what had happened.

CHAPTER 22

"Baby Boy and Baby Girl"

The first few days of January should have been full of joy and expectation; instead they proved difficult for us. Both of us were dogged with feelings of fear and anxiety about the future. At the same time, we were also doing our best to trust in God. In the early hours of the morning, on the ninth of January, I started getting some pains. We assumed this must be the start of labour. I felt scared of the hospital and the labour. I was wondering what would happen. That morning early, before breakfast, Bruce took me to the hospital. I was immediately admitted onto a ward in the maternity department. But as the day progressed, the pains eased up and stopped. Now I became anxious and restless, wanting to escape from the ward and go back home. Later that day, Bruce arrived to visit me, and to his surprise and dismay, he found me standing at the top of the staircase to the maternity wards, wearing only a nightdress with a coat on top. I was nervous and shaky, and I looked upset and forlorn. Bruce went up to the ward and spoke to a nurse. Apparently I had not yet gone into proper labour, and I was free to go back home, where I spent the night. But, in the early hours of the following morning, the pains began all over again. We went to the hospital again in the morning, and this time, the labour pains were coming in earnest. The midwife informed us that she expected the baby to be born later that same afternoon. However, by late evening, there was still no baby! I was feeling exhausted by now, so I was taken for an "epidural" in my back. This was a procedure to reduce or eliminate pain. The labour pains had died down, even though I was nearly three quarters of the way dilated. So the nursing staff had to induce labour again. Thankfully, I was able to get two or three hours of rest at that time.

Around midnight, the midwives became aware that the baby was in distress and in danger to its' life. The baby had become trapped, high up in the birth canal, with it's head in a sideways position. A major drama was unfolding before us. By this point, I was both mentally and physically exhausted; I began to despair of my baby ever being born. Despite all efforts, the baby was making no progress, and both mother and baby were growing weaker all the time. Bruce and I were crying out to God silently. The senior midwife made a decision; she made an emergency call, asking for an off-duty maternity doctor to come as quickly as possible. Within just a few minutes, a small oriental doctor hurried in. He made a quick examination of me, asking the midwives questions at the same time. He was visibly angry with the midwife and her staff, and said,

"Why did you not call me much earlier? I was on duty earlier this evening. Now you are forcing me to do a "high forceps" delivery, when this situation calls for a C-section. I have to get this baby out quickly! He may only last another five minutes."

All this was very frightening to us. In haste, and rather roughly, the doctor had to reach inside me with long forceps, which he gripped around the baby's head. With a lot of force, and a twisting action, he was able to dislodge the baby. Bruce and the nurses held my arms, while the doctor used all his diminutive weight and strength to pull the baby out. This was a very unpleasant experience for me; I felt like I was having my insides pulled out. Thankfully, the baby was still alive, but weak and in a state shock. This baby boy was placed on my chest, but I was too exhausted and shocked to respond to him. He was cleaned up and placed in a cot with a glass top, and he lay there very still with his eyes wide open. We named this baby David. Sadly, there was little opportunity for any bonding contact with him.

Next day, late in the afternoon, I was changing the baby's nappy. I had tried more than once to bottle-feed him, but he seemed unable to take the milk. Suddenly I noticed that his face was changing shade to a purple/blue colour. I was alarmed and looked around for help. An older midwife was walking past the window to the ward. I called out to her and she came straight over.

I said, "Look! There's something wrong with my baby!"

She took one look, and grabbed little David from me.

"Where are you taking him?" I asked, as she hurried away.

"Please don't follow me," she said quickly. "It'll be O.K."

Of course, I did try to follow, but I couldn't walk very fast because of my stitches. However, I saw her go into a room; in her haste, she left the door open a little. By the time I reached the place, I could see that she had put a tube down the baby's throat, and she was sucking out something. This turned out to be the mucus he had swallowed at his birth. Somehow, this vital procedure, which should have been done immediately after his birth, had been overlooked. The midwife saw me looking in, and waved her arm to try to make me go away. But I wouldn't go. So, when she had finished, she brought David out to me. Already his normal face colour had returned, and from that time onwards, David started to feed normally.

A few days later, mother and baby came home. I was unhappy in hospital, and I had started making plans to escape back home. I had been having great difficulty in sleeping, and was given medication. Fortunately, the consultant could see how restless and agitated I was, and he allowed me to come home with the baby. It took me at least six weeks to recover from the trauma, the bruising and the stitches. Thankfully, Bruce was able to help me with the baby and household chores, as he was not working.

It was nearly a year before Bruce was able to work again, as he had experienced a considerable blow to his confidence. He was experiencing anxiety and depressive symptoms. At last, he was offered a twelve-month contract to work at the local council offices on a community scheme. Just before Christmas, we were rather shocked to discover that I had become pregnant again. We felt this baby would be rather soon after the first one. But, in February I had to hurry to the doctor, as I was having severe stomach pains. The doctor sent me to the hospital for tests, where I was told that I had lost this baby through a miscarriage. They had to perform a procedure on me. When I returned home, I felt like a black cloud was hanging over me. I knew I had lost a child that I had never seen. There was a sense of depression and loss. Some Christian friends tried to comfort me. They assured me that this baby had been taken straight to Heaven; one day we would meet him or her up there. This did help me somewhat. Meanwhile I had to get on with caring for David, and this was not an easy task. He had a great fear of being left alone and of going to sleep. Bruce and I spent much time trying to comfort him and settle him off to sleep, and this continued through childhood. Sometimes we would walk the streets with him in his pram trying to settle him, only to have him wake again when we tried to transfer him to his bed.

In June, I discovered that I was expecting again. The baby would be due the following February, by which time David would be two. Bruce and I were pleased and more at peace now, but we had to pray daily that the baby would go safely to full term. Even with these prayers, I had a scare in the month of October. While attending a family christening one Sunday, I started to bleed. We came home as soon as we could, and I went to the doctor next morning. He reassured me that I was still carrying the baby, and told me to take things easy for a couple of days. The months went by, and I prayed every day for the safety of the baby inside. Meanwhile, David was now a toddler, walking and starting to talk. He loved to watch the trains. I would often take him to a bridge near our home, overlooking the main line from London Waterloo.

Christmas-time came and then New Year; time was getting close for this baby to be born. One day in late January, I took David to watch the trains. Suddenly, thick black clouds closed in, and it started to sleet and hail. David became frightened. I had to run back to the house, pushing him in his pushchair. Later that evening, at bedtime, my waters suddenly broke; I knew I had to get quickly to the hospital. A friend came over to be with David while Bruce took me to the hospital. I was admitted, and the staff there expected the baby to be born sometime the following day. They offered me a sleeping pill, but I refused this, and by the early hours I asked to be taken down for an epidural. After examining me, the midwife telephoned Bruce at home, asking him to come. Bruce arrived at about four o'clock in the morning. Already, the delivery was well advanced. Thankfully, this baby was not stuck. Before five o'clock that morning, I had given birth to a healthy baby girl. Bruce had been with me to witness the wonder of a normal birth. We named the baby Esther, being the second of the two names that we had received from the Lord. This time, I only had to spend one day and night in hospital, before I was allowed home. I did suffer with some mental problems, but not as severe as I had suffered with David. The consultant advised me against having any more children. Once I was back home, I recovered more quickly.

Meanwhile, Bruce's one-year contract had been extended by a few months, which afforded us some stability and income. When the contract did finish, Bruce was able to do some temping jobs for an agency, followed by part-time employment for a person in the church, doing bookkeeping for his carpet business.

CHAPTER 23

"Dark times ahead!"

David was now three years old and Esther was one. There were signs that Bruce was becoming increasingly unwell. He went to a doctor, who prescribed tranquillizers and then sleeping pills; followed on subsequent visits by more of the same. But these drugs didn't seem to help Bruce. I tried to get help from the church, but no one seemed to know what to do to help us. In desperation, we took a trip to a Christian businessmen's conference in the south east of France, hoping and praying that God would do a miracle for Bruce. By the end of the conference, nothing significant seemed to have taken place, so I approached an African man for help, and he quickly rallied a group of black Africans around Bruce. They prayed loudly in tongues and prophesied over Bruce and also over little David. Sadly though, Bruce could not respond to these prayers and by October, Bruce was worse still. Eventually, the pills seemed to be operating in reverse, and he went for over two weeks without any sleep at all, either by day or night. This was a very frightening time for me, as well as for Bruce. Even though he was not sleeping, Bruce was still trying to walk to and from his job each day. It was only a ten-minute walk, yet

Bruce would struggle home feeling exhausted. He tried to pray in tongues, but nothing seemed to lift the stress and anxiety within. When he reached the house, he found it difficult to communicate with any of the family. He was tired, stressed, irritable, snappy, and depressed. He began to shout at the children because they were noisy. Bruce would keep repeating the words "I am bad, I am bad", and he started having thoughts of suicide. Not wanting to leave us behind because we needed him, he began to talk about taking us all in the car and driving at speed over a cliff or into a motorway bridge. Bruce could no longer go to his job, and took to his bed most of the time. In desperation, I tried to seek help from various friends and organisations, but I was given conflicting advice. I felt that my family was collapsing, and I didn't know what to do to stop it. I prayed a lot and cried out to God in my heart.

On about the thirteenth day, we both went together to see the vicar. He looked very concerned, but didn't take any action. Instead, he suggested that we spend an hour together offering a sacrifice of praise and worship to God. We did our best to obey these instructions, despite the state we were now in. That evening we listened to a "Living Sound" album while I tried to get the children ready for bed. This wasn't easy, as they were both getting very upset and disturbed by the atmosphere in our house. At last, Bruce and I tried singing some worship songs, to Bruce's guitar. We kept this up for an hour or so, until Bruce felt exhausted and desperate. Where was God? Had he deserted us? We had longed for a spiritual breakthrough of some sort, but nothing had come. Exhausted and defeated, both mentally and physically,

Bruce went up to the bedroom while I went to one of the children's bedrooms, trying to give Bruce some space and peace. Bruce had been experiencing a constant drumming noise in the back of his neck, which prevented him from relaxing and sleeping. Now he experienced a visitation from the demonic forces of darkness. Though he saw nothing, he heard a voice within telling him,

"Now you have totally failed in every way. You can no longer call yourself a Christian; now you belong to Satan's side."

The voice also told him to expect some terrible things to happen, and that he himself was now destined for Hell, with no means of escape or redemption. Bruce even felt something turn over inside his stomach. The next morning, I woke up, having slept in one of the children's bedrooms. I went downstairs and found a suicidal letter waiting for me. I looked for Bruce, but could not find him anywhere; in a panic I ran to the curate's house for help. On arriving there, out of breath and very frightened, I was given a rebuke for leaving the children alone in the house, asleep in their beds. Then I was offered a lift home, and thankfully, I found the kids still fast asleep. At that moment, Bruce came back into the house through the back door, looking pale and scared. He had been walking the streets in a state of fear and apprehension. In his exhausted condition, he had believed the lying words that had been sown into his heart. He truly felt that he was bad and a complete failure, and that God had no further use for him. Soon the vicar arrived at our house, urging Bruce to go to a Christian healing retreat about thirty miles away. Then he said to me that it now seemed obvious that Bruce could not cope with married life or children. He suggested to me that we should consider separation or divorce, allowing Bruce to go back to his former way of life. This comment, though meant sincerely, cut me to the core. With my mind reeling in desperation, I grabbed the children and ran off to a park. I was crying out to God in my heart, wondering how all of this had been allowed to happen. I decided to build a wall of protection around my children and myself. I vowed that I would not allow anyone to come near us again or tell us what to do. My life and my security were under threat. I even thought I would never go near a church again.

Bruce's father had been contacted by phone and soon arrived at the house, to take Bruce away with him to his own house. I was able to speak to Bruce there by phone that evening, and I could tell from the fear in his voice that he did not want to be there. I had received a visit from an American lady, who I had met just once or twice before. I had an uneasy feeling about her, but she was persistent, almost forceful. I was extremely vulnerable, and she said that she was willing to snatch Bruce from outside his parent's house, and drive him to the West Country to see Luther and Sandy. They believed that Bruce needed deliverance prayer, and that they could help. So, the plan was hatched, and Bruce was snatched outside the house, and taken by car to see Luther and Sandy. However, it became quickly evident to them that the problem was more complex than a deliverance prayer. Meanwhile, Bruce's father was pressing me by telephone, to tell him where Bruce had been taken, even though Luther and Sandy did not wish him to know just yet. Eventually, Bruce's father and stepmother drove to the West Country and arrived at Luther's house. But

Bruce had been whisked away by the American lady from under their noses, and was on his way home again. By the time he arrived back home, Bruce was looking rather like a living corpse, and was complaining of a taste like death in his mouth.

That evening, Bruce's father had also arrived back from the West Country. Soon he came to our home, accompanied by one of the doctors from the local practice. This doctor looked very sympathetic and concerned. He took a quick look at Bruce, and announced that he had already arranged for Bruce to be admitted straight away to a private psychiatric hospital about fifteen miles away. I was asked to pack a few basic things for Bruce to take, and Bruce was driven away by his father to the hospital. I was now left alone with the children. I felt exhausted, both emotionally and physically, and I wondered what the future would hold. I felt I had nobody to turn to anymore, but I was relieved that Bruce was somewhere where he could be looked after. I did receive support and hospitality from Bruce's brother, Andrew, and his wife. They were horrified at what had happened, and they took us to their home, for walks, for a swim, and to visit Bruce in hospital. Using powerful drugs, the hospital had succeeded in getting Bruce to sleep, so his appearance was improving. However, he was still in a state of fear, finding it difficult to eat, and he had difficulty in relating with us.

Meanwhile I had two major things to deal with, neither of which I shared with anybody else. Firstly, I was receiving accusations from some ladies in two local churches. They had noticed that David, who was now about three and a half, was acting abnormally in playgroup, and they suspected possible child-abuse. They had also reported these suspicions to the doctor's surgery, and as a result, I had a phone call from my doctor, telling me that I was to receive a visit from a health visitor and a social worker. My doctor was angry and upset, and assured me that he did not believe these accusations. Never the less, the ladies came and observed David in the home. Afterwards, they felt satisfied that nothing improper had happened to David, and that he was probably reacting to Bruce's illness and absence. Never the less, a decision was made that David should now attend a playgroup for children with special needs. Although we went there for a year or more, neither David nor I enjoyed it very much. I also felt as if I was under observation, and I found this threatening.

Bruce was away in hospital for about ten weeks, during which time I managed reasonably well, though I stopped going to church, because I felt threatened by the people there. I felt that nobody seemed to have anything good to say about Bruce or I at that time. However, the American lady came a few times to visit me in her car, and took the children and I on outings and shopping. I needed the support of a mother figure in my life, and nobody from my family seemed to be there for me. So, at that time, the American lady seemed to be a wonderful friend. After Bruce had been in hospital for a few weeks, the diagnosis for his recovery was very poor. I was told that he would never work again. I received a phone call from his father, saying that he wanted to see me and talk to me. I felt rather numb inside, so I was not unduly frightened. He wanted me to go the next day, and he had even

arranged for Bruce's stepsister to collect the children and
I. She had also been asked to look after my children
while I was talking to Bruce's father. I had no idea what
was coming. When I arrived, I was invited into the sitting
room, where Bruce's father was sitting in his usual
armchair, alone in the room. Bruce's stepmother was in
the kitchen. I had noticed her there as I passed through
the hallway, and saw that she looked sad and maybe a
little tearful. I entered the sitting room and was asked to
sit down on another armchair. Bruce's father began to
speak about Bruce's illness, and he asked me what I
thought about the diagnosis. I told him that I had faith
that Bruce would recover over a period of time. I believe
that God was giving me faith and hope in my spirit,
when everyone around was looking at the present with
an attitude of gloom, seeing only disaster ahead. I
believed that God called us together, and he had a plan
and purpose for our lives. I did not want to be the one to
break that plan. After a short discussion, I could see that
Bruce's father still believed that Bruce would never func-
tion again as a family man. He felt it would be better for
everyone concerned for Bruce to go back to his former
way of life. Having said this, Bruce's father produced his
chequebook, and then made an offer to me. This
consisted of a very large sum of money, for me to bring
up the children, and a small house to live in. All this was
on condition that I would agree to let Bruce go, and
divorce him. The children and I were never to see Bruce
or anyone from his family again. As soon as Bruce's
father had finished speaking, I replied immediately
to him.

"No, I'm sorry. I can't do that. I married Bruce for
better or for worse. In any case, I don't believe that

this is what Bruce would want. I think it would finish him off."

The words seemed to come out of my mouth with sincerity, strength and conviction. To my relief, Bruce's father replied; "O.K. I admire you for your loyalty. I accept what you say. But if you change your mind, the offer still stands, and you know where to find me."

I was then given a lift home again with the children, feeling rather shocked by what had happened.

After a few weeks had passed, Bruce was allowed home for Christmas. He had already been home for a weekend. Bruce tried to adjust to family life, but was still struggling with the belief that he was going to hell. This continued for two or three months, while I tried to carry on with family responsibilities as best I could. By March, Bruce was going downhill again; it was decided that he should be re-admitted to hospital.

CHAPTER 24

"Darkness and Light"

It was very disappointing for us that Bruce had to go
back to hospital. But, on the plus side, he did not seem
to be as seriously ill as the first time. While Bruce was
in hospital, I telephoned a Christian organisation,
whose aim and purpose was to help and encourage ho-
mosexuals who had become Christians. They listened
carefully to me, and kindly suggested that one of their
members would be willing to visit Bruce in hospital. I
spoke to Bruce about this on my next visit, and he
agreed to receive a visit. It turned out that this visitor
was the brother of a man that Bruce already knew in a
Christian businessmen's organisation. A few days later,
Bruce received a visit from this young man, and he
went on to visit Bruce again, on more than one occasion. These visits proved helpful. The conversations began to give Bruce belief that he was still a Christian after all, and not beyond all hope. The young man
explained to Bruce that there were many others who
were struggling in a similar way; also there were conferences and other resources to help bring change and
healing. This was encouraging to Bruce, and to me; but
it would still take time to see real improvement in

Bruce's condition. Bruce had been given electric shock treatment at least three times on his first hospital stay, to try to lift the depression. This time, the psychiatrist decided to try treatment with Lithium, which is often used for treating chemical imbalances and mood disorders. Over a period of a few weeks, Bruce was showing signs of improvement, and he was allowed out of hospital after about eight weeks in total. I had been looking after the house and the children; during this period I had received few visitors.

When Bruce came home, he was still quite low, and he was taking various medications, which made him feel drugged. He told me that life through his eyes looked black and white only, without colour. It was arranged for Bruce to visit a Christian psychiatrist in London. We travelled by train as a family, and I entertained the children in a nearby park, while Bruce had his appointment. We had high hopes for these visits, but nothing much seemed to change, and Bruce felt that he was wasting everyone's time and money. By the autumn of that year, Bruce's father was purchasing a horticultural nursery, which was to be converted into a garden centre as part of the expanding family business. It was arranged that Bruce could go and help the existing owner, prior to the contracts being signed. Bruce would simply be pricking out seedlings in a greenhouse. At first, Bruce could only manage two hours of this work at most. However, a few weeks later, the purchase of the land had been made, and Bruce found himself working once again within the family business, albeit now at a fledgling garden centre instead of head office.

At long last, Bruce's health was steadily improving. Just before Christmas, we attended a carol service by candlelight. There was a Bible reading, followed by a carol, and this pattern was repeated several times. Bruce felt the presence of God coming over him every time a reading was given. This was the first time since his illness began that he had felt God's presence and heard God speak into his heart. Healing came more quickly now, and by the spring of the next year, Bruce could virtually work a normal day, with just a short lunchtime rest. He was able to do paperwork and administrative duties, serving customers, cashing-up of tills and banking of takings.

But now it was Mum who became ill again, and had to go back to hospital. [Miraculously, she had managed to go nine years since her previous period of illness.] We visited her on several occasions with the children, who found the hospital rather scary. We also took Sally and her family to visit. The doctors and social workers decided that Mum could no longer manage with a three-bedroom house, and she was offered a warden-controlled flat on her own. This meant that Richard and Jeffrey had to be moved from home to other accommodation.

After Christmas, we decided to put our house up for sale, and we bought a newer house on the edge of town. David was starting school in January, and we wanted a house located near the school. It also seemed right to leave behind the old house, which had been Bruce's bachelor pad before I met him. We felt God was telling us to make a new home together. We successfully moved between Christmas and New Year, and David started school a few days later. He seemed to settle in quite well.

I was still seeing the American lady; by now I had become rather over-dependent on her. Because of insecurity, vulnerability and loneliness, I had become attached to her as if she was my mother. She was twenty years older that me. Her husband was working but she was not, so she had time on her hands. She would come to the house quite often to help me with different things. She took the children and I on outings, and she even gave me driving lessons in her car. At this stage, this all seemed normal and very good, but unfortunately things were soon to change. About six months after our house-move, her husband was sent back to America with his job. She had to go with him. Her departure sparked off a deep rejection and insecurity in my life, which I found difficult to cope with. She was aware of this, and we spent a great deal of time and money speaking to one another on the phone. She even flew back to the U.K. four times over a period of a year and a half, staying with us each time, often for several weeks. During this period, I seemed more stable. I succeeded in passing my driving test. Esther started at school. However, when the American lady was not present with us, I would find myself sinking into times of despair and fear, resorting to self-harm with pills and alcohol, to dull my feelings of pain. I felt very black inside, and was unable to relate properly to the other family members. Hazel would sometimes come to visit me, and try to encourage me. There was also a new curate and his wife at the church who were very kind to me, and whom I appreciated very much. They would let me visit their house with David and Esther, as they had several children of their own, and they regularly gave us food.

But each time the American lady would return to stay with us again, our relationship became increasingly complicated, causing the family and I stress, confusion, shame and guilt. It became increasingly apparent that she had many problems of her own; and her views on how to help my family and I, often caused us more harm than good. It was all very upsetting and confusing to me, especially as I felt hopelessly bonded to her. Finally, on her last visit, things came to a head. In desperation, I had to seek help and advice from a Christian couple with experience in counselling. They exchanged words by telephone with the American lady, aimed at clearing up a few matters, but she became very angry and upset, and quickly packed her bags. She left our house to return home, and I have not seen her since. Although I wanted her to leave, the realisation that I would never see her again hit me very hard. I felt as if a knife had been thrust into me, and the pain would not go away. A few weeks later, while Bruce was out at an evening meeting and the children were in bed, I swallowed down a quantity of pills. They were powerful pills, prescribed for Mum, which we were looking after for her. After taking them, I went to bed. I was asleep when Bruce came in, so he knew nothing about what I had done. By the following morning I could not get up. I confessed to Bruce what I had done, and he immediately called a doctor. The doctor thought that I would be all right, but by that evening I was experiencing severe muscular problems and shaking. Bruce called for an ambulance, and I was taken to hospital. On admission to the casualty department, the duty doctor was horrified that so much time had gone by since I took the pills, and that the other doctor had not sent me to hospital. She said that they would do what they could, but it was really too late for treatment. Never the less, I was given antidote medication and I then lay awake all night with a nurse sitting by my bed holding my hand. I was very frightened, as my heart was racing at a dangerous speed. I was in real danger of heart failure, and I was praying to God to let me live. Thankfully, I made it through the night. By late afternoon on the following day, I was transferred to psychiatric hospital. It was the very same one where Bruce had been treated. However, because of my fear of hospitals, I only stayed there two or three days. I managed to convince the doctors that I was O.K. and promised not take pills like that again. They put me on anti-depressants, and I was allowed to return home. Once I was home, I struggled to cope with the house-work. The children did not want to go to school because they were scared to leave me on my own. David was having difficulties at school, but at this time we did not really understand why. In addition to all this, Mum was living alone in her flat, and was coming every Sunday to our house. We would take her to church and feed and care for her. I found this difficult, but felt obligated, as we had been doing this for her ever since we had been married, (except for the period when Bruce was in hospital). My sister, Sally and her family also visited regularly. She was no longer married, but she had two children of similar ages to mine, plus one more on the way. I would entertain them, feed them, and often transport them, since I now had the use of a car.

When the summer holidays arrived, we managed to attend a Christian summer camp. I found it difficult to feel part of it, but we did meet two young men there who had no homes to go back to, having been evicted from college due to drug taking. Both had recently committed their lives to Jesus, and Bruce and I felt moved by God to offer one of them a room in our house. Although this could have been a disaster, instead it proved a blessing on both sides, and we formed a good friendship. The other young man was also offered somewhere to live nearby, and both have since married and now have families of their own. During this period of having a lodger, one of my relatives phoned and begged me to take off them a six-month old black and white puppy called "Lady". We had already seen this dog a couple of times, and she was cute but very nervous. Bruce and I both love dogs, so we agreed to take her into our family. I collected her by car, and went to the pet shop to buy the necessary equipment and food. After that, I went to collect the children from school. They were both very excited to see Lady in the car, and to be told that she was now our puppy. However, our two-year old cat named Ziggy was considerably less thrilled to see this puppy on her patch. As Lady tried to investigate the stairs, having already eaten the cat food, she came face to face with Ziggy, and received a swipe of the paw across her nose. Lady was a nervous dog, and never tried to go near any cats again. When Bruce returned from work, he also made a big fuss of Lady. Later that evening, when the children were upstairs, Bruce and I spent time praying for the puppy, talking to her and stroking her. To our great relief, she settled into our house and family without the messing and behavioural problems, which we had been warned to expect. Over time, I found myself bonding emotionally with this dog, as a source of relief for my pain inside.

CHAPTER 25

"Time to Move"

Thankfully, the next two years proved to be rather more stable for us as a family. We continued to make our annual visit to the Christian summer conference, which was a particular highlight for us. We still had our lodger living with us during this period; it was often helpful to have another person around from time to time. Our son, David was still experiencing difficulties at school. His general behaviour was causing concern to his teachers, and also to us. He was not a bad boy, but he seemed unable to fit in with his peers, or with school requirements. On top of this, Esther was also having problems of her own at school, and was increasingly trying to stay off school, usually with sickness symptoms. We tried to find out what was going on, and she said it was because of verbal bullying. But our efforts to resolve matters at the school, seemed to come to nothing. So, after seeking God in prayer, I decided to offer myself for employment at the school as a lunchtime supervisory assistant. To my surprise, I was accepted for the post. I began to work there five lunchtimes per week. I enjoyed this work, and received a sense of worth from doing it. I was also able to keep a watchful eye on my own children in the playground, and they seemed happier, knowing I was there for an hour or so each day.

We were finding the costs of living very high. Our mortgage payments were increasing, as the whole country was going through a time of recession, with very high interest rates. After praying about our situation, we felt that God was telling us to move to a smaller house. Accordingly, we placed our house "For Sale" on the market, and started to view smaller houses. We went to view a three bedroom terraced house, and discovered that the owners wanted to move to a larger house. We liked their house and they arranged to view ours. They were happy with our house, so an exchange of properties was agreed. At that time, our lodger was also ready to move on, as he had become engaged, and was soon to be getting married. March arrived, and we moved to our new home; it was only a five-minute walk from our previous house, and slightly nearer to the school.

A short time later, I started going along to a Christian counselling ministry. I had to drive an hour's journey each way to attend my appointments, and these were spaced out, with several weeks in between. There was always a lot of talking and questions to answer; I also felt threatened by the fact that they were taking notes about me all the time. I found this method difficult to cope with, and when they did start to pray for me, it always seemed too short and not to reach my deep needs. Never the less, I kept going back over a period of nearly two years. Still, out of this, I did meet two very kind ladies called Maro and Marion, who had previously been connected with this ministry. Now they had taken a counselling room at the church we were attending. Their method of ministry was still very similar, and I soon gave up going along. However, Maro remained a friend to me, even to this day. She would often greet me when I arrived at the church, and she would put her arm around me and sit with me in the church. Ironically, I found this action more helpful to me than the counselling.

That same year, our son David was given a medical diagnosis via the child psychiatrist and psychologist. This entitled him to receive special help at school. It seems that his brain may have been deprived of oxygen around the period of his birth. All this helped us to understand David more, and to begin to ask God for healing for him. Also during this year, Bruce and I were able to attend a healing conference in the Midlands. Up to this point, my emotions had remained very dead, and prayer seemed to have little effect on me. However, at this conference, a lady started winking and smiling at me in the dining hall, both at the evening meal on the first night, and again at breakfast. I was attracted by this friendliness, but I was also unsure about her reasons for it. It turned out that this lady was one of the speakers at the conference, and her name was Mary. She spoke the following day, and at the end of her talk, she gave words of knowledge about a few people. She asked for these people to come forward. I was one of those who responded. As she prayed for me, she spoke "LIFE" into my emotions, which had been dead from early childhood. I felt a sensation like a bolt of electricity going through me, causing a shaking feeling in my inner being. This prayer was the start of my long road to recovery.

In the following year, David changed schools. He was now old enough to attend secondary school. At first he seemed to adjust quite well, and the school had an active special needs department. However, by the second year, he was not coping. Unsociable sleep patterns returned and he started staying off school. We tried all sorts of avenues to encourage him to go, but with little success. In some desperation, I made contact with a school support worker. As it turned out, this person had known me as a child and had tried to help me. Now she made great efforts to support David in getting him to school. She was not always successful, but he attended enough to attain reasonable grades in the GCSE exams.

The main part of the family business had entered difficult times in the recession. Due to various factors, the business had to sell up. The garden centre was able to continue trading for a little longer, but a buyer also had to be found. In time, a buyer came along, who promised to retain all existing staff members. However, once these new owners took control, they looked for ways to push Bruce out, probably because he was part of the former ownership. Bruce worked for them for six weeks, including six weekends, before he was dismissed. They told him that they had discovered he had previously been mentally unwell, and they felt that he would not be able to work at their new pace. Even though there was a redundancy cheque for Bruce, this was a major blow to us as a family. Thankfully, we felt encouraged by God the following weekend, when we attended a prayer weekend. During this, God told us that he had everything under control, and we must continue to trust him. On our return, Bruce was accepted by an employment agency, and he was able to do some temping work over the next few months. After this, Bruce successfully applied for a year's contract, working for a "High Street" branch of a large bank; they were preparing to move to a new call centre the following year. The work proved challenging at first, but with perseverance Bruce was able to cope with it. Meanwhile, I was gradually growing stronger in myself, and I was more able to receive from God at conferences. Each summer, we would attend the summer camp, where Mary would always be, conducting a seminar. Without fail, I would receive some healing and blessing at these. We also continued to attend local church regularly. But I still suffered with the sense of being misunderstood, and of not being fully accepted. This made it difficult for me to receive from God, especially in my own hometown.

Meanwhile Mum had spent nearly three years living in her flat. But recently she had been finding life increasingly difficult on her own, and was not coping very well. I was now visiting her daily, and we would have her round to our house every weekend. In the early days of living in her flat, she had managed to invite us round as a family, and even cook a roast dinner for us. But by now things were not so good, and I could see the warning signs I knew so well. One evening, I was getting myself ready for bed, when I felt an urgent sense that I should go round to her flat. I obeyed and drove the ten-minute journey there. When I arrived, I found Mum in the bath, trying to drown herself. I pulled out the plug to empty the bath and kept talking to her, whilst also managing to call an ambulance and Bruce. The ambulance arrived, and Mum was taken to hospital, where she stayed for nearly a year. During this time, the authorities found her a place in a residential care home, to replace her flat. Later on, when she finally came back out of hospital, she settled in very well in this home, being the youngest person there at just sixty-five years old.

Meanwhile, Bruce completed his year of work at the bank. He had started looking for something else, when his father obtained an introduction for him to a lady who ran an Estate Agency business in the town. It was agreed that Bruce would join the firm as a general trainee, and he started there after Christmas. At first it seemed rather boring and unproductive, as Bruce was given little to do. But after a few months, Bruce was moved to their other branch, a few miles away. Here he related well with the young manager, and rapidly picked up the ropes and gained experience and success. Now Bruce was in a job that was giving him satisfaction, with the opportunity to grow in self-esteem.

Our daughter, Esther had now started at secondary school. As a sensitive person, she again became the target of verbal bullying right from the start. After a few months, she started feigning illnesses almost every morning and refusing to go to school. This caused me considerable stress and anxiety, and my own mental health started to suffer. After about a year, we managed to get Esther into a nearby private Christian school. Here she soon became much happier, and began to make some new friends. During that summer, we made a trip to Devon with the family, and we took Mum along with us. Mum still had some relatives living in Devon, so this was an opportunity for her to see them. [We hoped that a trip to Devon would do her good, as she had recently been admitted from her care-home to the general hospital, suffering with a serious bladder infection.] Once we were in Devon, we visited the local Zoo, and various other attractions. A highlight for Mum was that she was able to spend an evening with her brother, and have a meal with him. She had been very excited about this, and enjoyed it very much. [This was the brother who was deaf and dumb, and had visited many years before in the three-wheeler car.]

At the end of that year, Mum spent Christmas day with us, and she seemed to have a good day and to have enjoyed herself. However, during the weeks that followed, she started to become sullen and quite depressed. Out of the blue, one morning, I received a phone call to say that Mum had been admitted to the local psychiatric unit. [The hospital she used to attend had now been closed down.] I visited her regularly, but I was not happy with the situation, because she was not showing her usual symptoms of mental illness. After every visit, I would ask to see the doctor in charge; he would always blame her behaviour on an overactive thyroid. He would then tell me that she could not go back to her care-home, but that they would have to find another place for her to live. I could not understand why this was at the time, as Mum had settled in so well there. As time went by, Mum became more and more physically unwell. I was convinced she had a chest infection. She was making a rattling sound in her chest or throat, which was getting worse on every visit. This concerned me greatly, but every time I raised the matter with the staff, I was always assured that she was being properly treated, and that everything was under control. However, when I visited her again a week or two later, she could hardly speak; she seemed to be trying to say that she needed help, because they were killing her. I put this down to her mental health, deteriorating with her physical health. A few days later, on the last occasion that we visited her at this hospital, Bruce and I found her slumped in a chair, barely conscious. We were both very alarmed and I rushed to find a member of staff. I asked for my Mum to seen by a doctor in the Casualty department of the nearby general hospital. I even considered pushing her in a wheelchair up the long steep hill to the main hospital, but she was too unresponsive to be able to move her in this way. Meanwhile, the staff assured me that a doctor had been called, and that he was on his way. I believed this, and we had to leave, as visiting hours were now over.

The following morning I took the children to school. When I returned, I had an inner sense that something was seriously wrong with Mum. I arranged for a neighbour to look after Lady, my dog, and I was just about to go to the car to drive to the hospital, when the telephone rang. This call turned out to be from the Casualty department. They were asking that I come to the hospital as soon as possible. I hurried to the hospital, and after parking the car, I arrived at Casualty. I was taken into a side room, where I was asked to wait. The nurse told me that I could not see my mother because she was receiving treatment, and that someone would be with me shortly to tell me what was happening. I was very restless and anxious, and once or twice I wandered around the casualty department. At one point I even passed the cubicle where she was receiving emergency treatment, but I did not realise that it was Mum. Eventually, at least an hour later, a lady doctor came to me.

"Are you Joan's eldest daughter, her next of kin?" she asked.

"Yes I am," I replied.

"I'm very sorry to have to tell you that your Mum is a very poorly lady. Her heart stopped in the ambulance on the way here, and I have been working hard for fifteen minutes to get her heart going again. We have succeeded in stabilising her, and we will be moving her up to Intensive Care as soon as we can. This is a delicate and lengthy procedure, so please be patient with us. Once she is settled there, then you can see her."

"Is she going to make it?" was all I could ask.

"Again I say to you that your Mum is a very poorly lady, and I cannot answer that question at this stage. We will have to see," the doctor replied.

I felt dazed and shocked, and angry with myself that I had not been with Mum when she had the cardiac arrest. Never the less, I managed to phone the other members of my family, to tell them to get to the hospital as soon as possible. I did get to see Mum at about two o'clock; she was in the Intensive care department. She was connected up to a life-support machine, and she showed no apparent signs of life. I was told that she was fully sedated. By this time, Johnny, Sally, Richard and Jeffrey had all arrived, all in a state of shock and disbelief. Bruce was also there.

Over the next two or three days there was no change in Mum's condition. The consultant was asking me lots of questions about Mum's neglected condition, thinking that I was to blame for it. His notes even suggested that she had been admitted from a different local nursing home. Then it came to light that there were two patients, both with Mum's name and date of birth. He was shocked to discover that she had been in the psychiatric unit just down the hill. Then he explained to me that she had suffered with an overactive thyroid, but that this had not been treated in the correct manner. This had caused her to pick up a chest infection, which also had not been properly treated, and which had developed into double pneumonia. Eventually, her lungs had become so filled with fluid that the pressure in the lungs had caused her heart to stop. The consultant did not make a final prognosis, but the following day I asked an intensive care nurse,

"How am I supposed to cope with my Mum when she comes out, not being able to feed herself, or wash and dress herself?"

The nurse replied; "I'm sorry, but you won't need to cope with any of these things, because your Mum is going to pass away. I think you should talk to the consultant about the timing of it."

Again I felt shocked. When I did speak to the consultant, he said,

"We have done our best, but I'm afraid your Mum is brain dead; she is never going to recover. The kindest thing for all concerned is to switch off the life support machine, and let her pass away comfortably and peacefully."

So it was agreed with all the family that her support machine would be switched off on Monday morning. This was exactly one week after her cardiac arrest. Later that day, Mum's heart stopped beating, and she passed away peacefully to go to be with Jesus. A week later, her funeral took place in the church she had attended with our family. We sang some of her favourite songs, our son David read the lesson, and Esther and her cousins wrote and read out a poem about her.

Just for the record, over the following months, after receiving legal advice, we did make a complaint about the negligent treatment that Mum had received at the psychiatric unit. This was a lengthy and painful process, as it involved looking into files and notes about her, going back over many years of treatment. The whole process caused me considerable pain, stress and grief. However, in the end, there were reprimands for the staff involved, and changes were made for the better treatment of future patients. We ourselves received a modest amount of compensation, which was shared between all five of Mum's children.

CHAPTER 26

"Heart Attack"

A few months had passed since Mum's death, but I was still feeling numb and vulnerable inside. Although I fully realised that my relationship with Mum had been lacking in very many ways, yet deep within me there was still a great need for a mother. I believe this is called a "mother wound". About this time, I met a woman who attended the same church home group as me. One day she invited me to come round to her house for a coffee. I agreed to go, and decided to walk to her house, as it was nearby. I took my dog, Lady, along with me. Alice, as she was called, told me that she had recently lost her dog, so she made a big fuss of Lady. I always felt safer with people who liked my dog; so over the following months, I allowed Alice to become a friend, both to me, and my family. She came to our house for food, went on outings, including an occasional trip to the cinema. Alice had never been married and lived on her own. She had plenty of time to spare.

Over time, Lady, our dog, was deteriorating significantly. By now she was seven years old, and over the last three years had been getting increasingly lame. Now she struggled to get up stairs; even walking itself was becoming difficult, as her back legs could carry little weight. We made several visits to local vets, all of whom did not know what the problem was. Once or twice, they suggested to us that Lady be put to sleep, but I refused this advice rather indignantly. Finally, maybe in desperation, one vet referred us to the Bristol University Vet Training School at Langford. In so doing, they commented that we would be wasting our time and money. We made the trip to Langford as a family, on the first occasion. A middle-aged gentleman in a white coat, who turned out to be the senior professor at the training college, examined Lady. We were impressed by his caring attitude as well as his obvious knowledge about animals. He explained that the problems were mostly in the brain, and that he wanted to take her on as a "Research" case, to help advance veterinary science. Because her symptoms were difficult to diagnose, he told us that most of the future treatment would be carried out free of charge. He explained to us that he could not promise a cure. However, he assured us that he would do all in his power either to cure her or at least to prolong her life. Finally, he asked cautiously if, when she finally passed away, he could to keep her body for a post-mortem investigation. We agreed to this request, as we could tell that he was a very caring, sincere and compassionate person, who wanted to do his very best to help animals.

Over the following year, I had to make several trips to Langford with Lady. By now, Bruce had been given the opportunity to purchase and run his own estate agency branch in a village about seven miles from our home. As it was now difficult for Bruce to take time off work, Alice offered to drive me to Langford with Lady on several occasions. She had become a loyal and trusted friend, who seemed willing to do almost anything to help me. When summer came, we were given special permission to take Lady with us to the Christian summer camp, on account of her disabilities and medication. Alice also came with us to the camp, to help me with Lady and do some dog sitting. I felt very fortunate to have her around.

During the springtime, Bruce and I had been feeling strongly that the Lord wanted us to move house. We found a house about seven miles from where we were living. The new house was very near both to Bruce's office and also to Esther's school. We completed the move very soon after the summer camp. Although I believed that the move was God's will, and I could see the benefits of it, yet I still felt very insecure and homesick for a year or so afterwards. This caused me to cling more to Alice, and to become very dependent on her. We had joined an Anglican church in the village, and gradually were beginning to get to know a few of the people there. But because of my insecurity and fears, Alice would come over to attend the evening service with me, acting rather like a protection or security shield. Looking back now, I realise that this was not helpful for me, as it hindered me from making new friendships. But at the time it all seemed to be for the best. I did get myself a little job, as a lunchtime supervisory assistant, at the nearby secondary school. But it proved very different from the previous job at a junior school, and I didn't stay there very long.

After three years of visiting Langford, Lady had gradually deteriorated to the point that she could no longer walk un-aided, despite various medications. We had to take her around in a pushchair for her walks, and lift her out to do her "business". However she had still had some quality of life, and did not seem to be suffering pain. Eventually though, it came to the point when we had to agree with the professor that her quality of life had become very poor, and she should be quietly put to sleep. She had already lived a few years longer than the other vets had predicted. So, the whole family, together with Alice took our final trip to Langford with Lady. We were all permitted to be in the room with her while she received the injection. Bruce held her paw and stroked her back, speaking softly to her and praying for her as he watched her pass away peacefully. As for me, I couldn't cope with it like Bruce did. Instead, I just stood in a corner with my body shaking, unable to watch or even say anything. I felt like something was being ripped out of me, but I could not express my feelings of loss and grief. The long journey home seemed awful to me, and by the next day, I had to call the doctor, as I couldn't stop shaking. The doctor was very understanding and prescribed some medication to calm my nerves. Soon afterwards, we decided to take a holiday to France. This helped me to have something else to think about, and to adjust to life without Lady. When we came back, I decided to offer myself to the local dog rescue centre as a casual dog walker. I soon found myself wanting to take some of the rescue dogs back home with me, but of course, we still had Ziggy living at home, who by now was getting an older cat.

My son David had been learning to play the guitar and the bass guitar, and the opportunity arose for him to be involved with the worship at church, and later to be part of a Christian worship band. David also sang with this band, and they played at some church events in the area. One such event took place in the local village, and the visiting preacher was called Steve. He had overcome a hard life, and now was strong in his faith. There was a presence of the Holy Spirit at each of the meetings at which he was speaking, and the mission lasted for two weeks. Each night there were also opportunities to receive personal prayer, and I went forward on more than one occasion. As Steve prayed for me, I was touched by God, and I received some emotional healing from these prayers. This was a continuation of God's work in my life. After these meetings were over, I began to meet up with the vicar's wife once a fortnight for a coffee, a chat and a prayer. She would sit next to me on the sofa and put a comforting arm round my shoulders. She would continue like this for half an hour or so, while we talked and prayed, and again I would find this both meaningful and healing. Another lady in the church joined with us. Having received some previous ministry training, she introduced her own ideas as to how to help me. Unfortunately, these actually became too complicated for my needs at that time, and I ceased to find the time helpful. After a little while, the meetings came to an end.

About five months after Lady had passed away, the family and I were all feeling the desire to have a dog again. We decided to look for a puppy, rather than an older dog. We visited one or two rescue centres, including the one where I helped with dog walking, to see if we could find the right dog for us. I already felt that God had told me the name for our next dog. The dog was to be called "Sam", but to start with we thought this would be the name of a female dog. As hard as we looked, we couldn't find Sam. Then one Saturday, we knew that this was the day to find the dog; Bruce had woken from a dream in which he had seen a brown and white dog on it's back with all four legs in the air. We had already planned to make a journey that morning to a dog sanctuary about twenty-five miles away, but when we arrived and searched excitedly round the place, it was all to no avail. There was no dog that fitted the description. We travelled back and arrived home feeling rather dejected in the early afternoon, wondering why we had felt so sure. At that moment, I remembered an advertisement I had seen for some pedigree puppies for sale, in the local newspaper. We had been expecting to take a rescue puppy, so I had actually thrown the paper in the dustbin. Now I had to fish it back out again. Bruce found the advert, which was for Springer Spaniel puppies, and nervously phoned the number. A man answered the phone.

"I only have one puppy left," he explained, "and he's a boy." He went on to say that he had already turned away some earlier callers, because he didn't feel that they were suitable for this particular breed. But as the conversation continued, he said that for some reason he liked the sound of Bruce's voice, and he invited us to come over to view the puppy in an hour or so. We all hurriedly got ready to make another trip, and we travelled excitedly over to the breeder's house, which was in a town about twenty miles away.

When we arrived, we saw the puppy's mother and grandmother in their garden. Both were very friendly, and were brown with some white parts. The older female rolled onto her bag for a stroke, with her legs in the air, just like in Bruce's dream. Then the puppy himself appeared. Although he was only about nine weeks old, he was so cute and friendly we all knew that this was the dog for us, even though he was a male puppy. During the visit, we got on very well with the breeder and his family, and a lot of things just fell into place. We were about to go on a holiday, and they were happy to keep Sam for two more weeks. On our return, we came excitedly to collect him. It wasn't long before we realised what a boisterous little puppy he was. Many shoes and other objects were chewed up, and most of the plants and shrubs in the garden got dug up. I took him to puppy classes for training, which was helpful in some areas. He retained the ability to embarrass us occasionally in public places by stealing things off people and running off with them. However he has now grown into a beautiful and emotional dog.

Three months later, Bruce and I had decided to take a prayer walk in a nearby country park on a Sunday morning in November. We had Sam with us. This park also had a miniature steam railway, which was open to the public. Bruce was complaining of feeling unwell, irritable and lethargic. We had to have Sam on his lead, because of the railway track. As we were approaching the railway, Bruce started complaining of chest pains, and we thought this was due to Sam pulling on his lead. The young spaniel was already surprisingly strong. However, after a few more minutes, the pain was getting worse, so I decided to take Sam myself, and make my way back to collect the car. I planned to take Bruce home and call a doctor for him. However, as I started to hurry, I slipped on some mud and wet leaves. I landed awkwardly half way down a bank, with shooting pains coming from my right leg. My leg had been twisted, and was now trapped underneath me. I called out in pain for help; then I saw Bruce trying to climb over a low wooden fence, and go staggering off down the road. After a few minutes, I managed to get to my feet, but I was still in pain. By now, I was sensing a great deal of urgency in my spirit. Somehow I managed to struggle over the low fence with Sam; just then I saw a woman with a teenage boy hurrying towards me up the road. "They were coming for me!" I thought. The boy took hold of Sam on his lead, while I had to lean on the shoulders of the lady. Together we hobbled to the small station building, which belonged to the miniature railway, which was about three hundred yards away. On the way, she had to break the news to me.

"I'm afraid your husband is having a heart attack," she said. "We have already used the phone at the miniature railway station to call for an ambulance."

As I arrived, I caught a glimpse of Bruce, lying on a timber bench gasping for breath. Then an ambulance arrived. Miraculously, this ambulance had been returning empty to a hospital about five miles away, and it was only a short distance away when the emergency call came through. Bruce was taken into the ambulance, and tests were done before he was taken to the General Hospital.

I was not allowed to go in the ambulance myself, but then a rapid response vehicle arrived. By now, Sam was very distressed. He was howling and whimpering with anxiety, aware that something frightening was happening. A paramedic came over to me and examined my leg. It had been badly twisted, but he didn't think it was broken. They wanted to take me to hospital for X-rays, but I explained that I could not abandon the dog. So they agreed to let me call a friend to take Sam and I home. I promised that I would go to the hospital later. I called Alice, and she came over in her car and took Sam and I home. When I arrived home, I was still in pain and shock. Alice told David what had happened to Bruce, and then went upstairs and told Esther. While we stopped for a cup of tea, I phoned Bruce's brother Andrew. He was rather shocked but he also assumed that I was exaggerating. He said he would come over to take us to the hospital. After quite a while had gone by, and I was fretting to get to the hospital, Andrew arrived at our house in his car. He took David, Esther and I to the hospital, while Alice stayed with Sam. At long last, we arrived at casualty, only to be told that Bruce had been moved to a "High Care" ward. I was told that Bruce had suffered a full heart attack on arrival, actually in the casualty department itself. He had received clot buster drug treatment, which had saved his life. Bruce had only just regained consciousness as we were entering the hospital. So we were only allowed to see him for a few minutes. Bruce looked very white, and was still feeling dazed, but he looked to be at peace.

Over the next week, the family and I went to visit Bruce several times. Esther brought a portable CD player into the hospital, with two of Bruce's favourite Christian music CD's. Over the next week, Bruce listened to them over the headphones whenever he had the strength, and he received great blessing and encouragement from the Lord. He told me that God had been very close to him, and had been speaking to him about the future. Apparently, in the ambulance, Bruce had prayed to say he was ready to come home to God, but would prefer to live as there was much still to do here.

Meanwhile, Alice came to help me at home, and moved in for about six weeks while Bruce was away. I was feeling very vulnerable, with feelings of grief and panic. Though Bruce was being blessed, I was feeling very insecure because the hospital staff had said at his admission that they did not know whether he would live or die. I couldn't cope with the idea of life without Bruce. I only shared these feelings with Alice, and not with anyone else. I was trying to be brave and strong for David and Esther, but meanwhile I was finding myself depending more and more on Alice, who was helping with driving, dog walking, cooking, washing up, etc. I was still unable to do a lot to start with, until my leg improved.

Back at the hospital, it was found that Bruce needed to have something called a "stent" fitted, in order to open up an artery, which was ninety percent blocked. After this procedure, Bruce was allowed out to convalesce, but because our house was too noisy and active, with children and a puppy, Bruce went to spend about three weeks, staying at his brother Andrew's house. Here it was peaceful and quiet, with no stress for him. Although Bruce was still quite weak, he continued to receive peace from God, and grew stronger each day. As for me, although I was able to visit Bruce quite a few times, I was still plagued by feelings of insecurity and vulnerability. In time Bruce was strong enough to come back home. Alice then returned to her own home, but she continued to visit us often, including spending Christmas Day with our family.

CHAPTER 27

"An Emotional Roller-Coaster"

Over the months that followed, through spring and into summer, the emotional dependency between Alice and I continued to grow like a climbing plant, almost to the point of suffocation. We were spending more and more time together, both in the daytime and the evenings. I felt I was becoming totally dependent on her. Yet, her presence around me seemed helpful in filling a deep need within me, which was unhealed at that time. Bruce and the children were forced to tolerate having an extra person in the home much of the time, almost standing between them and a distant me. Alice did try to take on the role of an Auntie to the children, taking them out from time to time with me. But, looking back, I can see that the stifling nature of the friendship was actually getting in the way of what God wanted to do in my life. I knew things could not continue like this much longer. Something was bound to change. But I didn't know how or when.

The days passed, and the atmosphere in the family was becoming increasingly difficult. Disagreements were creeping in; frustrations were showing. After several weeks of strained friendship, things came to a head. We had travelled as a group to the Christian summer camp. This year we had booked accommodation, and someone was looking after Sam for the week. Bruce and David were in one Guest House, and Esther, Alice and I were sharing a room in another Guest House, very close by. Certain circumstances caused a big upset during the night. Following this, Alice decided abruptly that she wished to end our friendship completely. Her decision hit me very hard. I was very emotionally vulnerable, and to me, this was like a complete rejection. It was as if all my old wounds were reopened. My head could understand what was going on, but my emotions were like those of a child; they could not understand or cope at all. Bruce and David found us in a state that morning, and we were forced to abort the whole week, making apologies to the two Guest Houses and paying what we owed them.

Over the weeks ahead, I was becoming increasingly emotionally and mentally unwell, despite the efforts of family and friends to help me. I made several visits to my doctor, who also made great efforts to support me in this crisis. During this period, I began to wander off on my own, often taking the car and usually taking the dog with me. I often took alcohol or pills with me, in an effort to numb my pain. Several times I found myself outside Alice's house, which was about seven miles from our home, and I had usually taken the alcohol and pills already. My desire and intention was to seek a reconciliation of the friendship. I longed to return to how things were in the days when I first knew her. Of course, instead of achieving reconciliation, my presence produced the opposite reaction. Receiving further rejection would provoke a desperate reaction from me; more than once, the police were called to deal with me. Yet, when they arrived, the police showed great concern about my state of mind. They treated me with kindness; they could plainly see that I was very distressed and mentally unwell. On one occasion, after I had received rejection again, in distress, I picked up a large flowerpot and threw it at Alice's house. It smashed through the window of the house. This had not been my intention, but now in fear and turmoil, I took out a packet of pills, which were in my bag. I somehow managed to swallow them all, even though I had nothing to drink them down with. I then ran away, frightened that the police would find me and arrest me. I ended up down by the river, about a mile away, still with the dog. I was lying on the ground feeling very drowsy, with a horrible taste in my mouth. I remember, as if in a fog, that Sam, my dog, was sitting by my head whimpering and licking my face, trying to keep me awake. Then I vaguely recollect two policewomen finding me there, by the river. They were asking me various questions.

"Are you O.K.? Can we help you? What's your' name?" etc.

Somehow I managed to tell them I had swallowed pills, and they asked if I still had the packet. I still had it; they took it from me. They helped me to their police vehicle, and put both Sam and I into it. I was taken straight to the hospital, where one of the policewomen stayed at my side for several hours. The other one took Sam back home, where Bruce was waiting, having received a phone call from the police at his office. I had taken a very dangerous overdose; I had to stay overnight in hospital, on a heart monitor and a drip.

In the days that followed, I was still far from well.

Meanwhile Bruce and I had started watching a program on the God TV channel, which was coming from a church in Toronto, Canada. This program proved comforting and hopeful to me. It gave me some hope of receiving healing in my dark situation. Bruce and I decided that we would try to find a way to get me to Toronto as soon as possible. I decided to go over there on my own, with my daughter Esther following three days later, after finishing her exams. At that point it was not possible for the whole family to go together, so Bruce had to stay behind, to look after David and Sam, and also to run his office. Bruce had phoned the church in Canada to explain the desperate situation with me. To our relief, they were compassionate towards me and offered to send a lady to meet me off the plane at Toronto airport. I was in a very fragile mental state, and only just made it through immigration control. But God gave me an inner peace and I was able to make the journey, and meet a lady that I didn't know. She was very kind towards me; she took me to my hotel and settled me into my hotel room. The next day, I made my way to the church on foot, about a ten- minute walk, and spent the whole day there. I met some more ladies there, and in the evening I received two hours of prayer from an older lady who was very kind and comforting to me. Through her love and prayers, God started to put me back together again. The following day, I received more encouragement by visiting their healing rooms, and prophesy rooms. Later on, people started arriving for the evening meeting. They were carrying pillows or cushions. I was baffled by this, and asked someone,

"Excuse me. Why is everybody bringing pillows to church? Are they all staying the night?"

The person smiled, and then explained that this was going to be a "soaking" meeting. Each person would find a place to sit or lie down where they felt comfortable. When the music and the words started, they were supposed to flow over you and into you, to minister peace and healing to your spirit as you soaked them in. Some kind person gave me a cushion, and I tried my best to lie still on the floor, like everyone else; but I was rather restless. Then, as the soaking got underway, a man who was leading the meeting came and knelt down beside me. He began to speak words of peace and encouragement to me from God. This was very helpful to me and I grew calmer. A few minutes later, a lady who had been singing and playing the violin, also came over to where I was lying. She stopped beside me and knelt down. She played her violin over me, and afterwards spoke some words of healing to me. Even though my emotions were still very ragged and raw, I felt a sense of heat going deep into my being, and peace and hope were beginning to return to me. The following day, Esther arrived, having successfully made the trip to Canada by herself. I felt well enough to meet her at the airport myself. During her stay, we went to some of the meetings together, but we also made a sightseeing trip into downtown Toronto. Esther was going through a difficult time herself, so it was hard for her to join in as I had done. But it was helpful for me to have her there as company. After a week, we both returned home.

Sadly, on our return home, we realised that our cat, Ziggy, had become very ill. She had kidney disease, and now it had advanced to kidney failure. We knew that the time had come for her to be put to sleep. This was particularly hard for Esther, who was very fond of the cat. Having returned home, I now found myself very alone in the church. Many people seemed to be avoiding me, perhaps because they did not know how to help me. However, I spent many hours talking with Hazel, mostly over the telephone. I also made contact with a lady called Sylvia, who I knew from a previous church, and she agreed to meet me from time to time for a coffee and a chat. This gave me some sense of worth and friendship. However, I was greatly missing what I had found in Toronto. Bruce and I prayed about this and we felt that God was prompting us to go back as a family, to spend more time there. We were able to find a local family to look after Sam, and we bought tickets for our family to travel back to Canada. When the time came, we duly arrived over there. Our first involvement was to attend their healing and prophecy rooms. We were all amazed and encouraged at the words spoken to each of us. The church was also hosting four evenings with a visiting Canadian evangelist. He was a young man, who had come from a rough background, but was now very anointed by the Holy Spirit. We were helped and encouraged by his dynamic Bible teaching and his faith. During the services, we also witnessed powerful praise and worship, and we saw healings taking place in other people's lives. We ourselves received impartations each night through the laying on of hands. In all of these things, I was feeling myself opening up more to the Holy Spirit, and I was getting stronger in my own spirit. I felt the rejection was diminishing, and I was gaining a new hope and a stronger faith in God. I was learning to give things over to the Lord, and allow him greater control of my life.

We spent two weeks over there, and God did work in the lives of the whole family. We returned home in November, with various teaching and soaking materials, which we soon began to listen to at home. Once back home, a friend called Gay, started to join us, coming quite often to our home for a soaking evening with the family. We shared meals together from time to time at either of our houses, and Gay also came along with us to some conferences we attended more locally.

However, after Christmas and New Year had passed, I was finding myself slipping back into feelings of fear and isolation. Though the time in Canada had been so uplifting, it all seemed a long way off now, and I was still experiencing a lack of help and support. My doctor continued to be very caring and faithful, even calling at my home unexpectedly more than once. However, the church and home group we attended struggled to understand my continuing needs, especially as I had become restless and agitated once again. However, there was one lady that I noticed at home group, and I received a sense in my spirit that she would become a good friend. Likewise, unknown to me, she had also felt the same sense about me. She could see that I needed support, and that I wasn't receiving any. This lady, whose name was Lily, showed compassion towards me, and we arranged to meet at her home for a coffee. She confessed later on to feeling quite nervous before my first visit. However, all went well, and I began to meet Lily on a regular basis. We would play board games, and make little outings together to a garden centre or to the shops in town. It was helpful to me having a faithful friend who felt safe to me. Lily had been a nurse for many years until her retirement; she had three grown up children, and several grandchildren.

During that year, as I was regaining strength once more, we heard about a church near Birmingham which was hosting conferences with international speakers, rather like in Toronto. We decided to travel up there in April and stay for four nights, in order to attend a conference. The main speaker was that same young man whom we had seen before in Canada. The worship was anointed, but even so, I found that I needed a lady to sit with me, because fear and agitation were still trying to attack me and make me run out. I received some further healing through the impartation of laying-on of hands. Soon after, we became partners with the ministry of this young evangelist, and they provided a prayer-line phone number for people to ring. I was still regularly experiencing problems, being hounded by an overwhelming fear. I would pray against this myself and call out to Jesus for help on many occasions. Then I telephoned the prayer line in Canada; a lady there was very helpful to me. I spoke to her several times over the following months, and she led me through repentance regarding open doors that I had given to the enemy by negative things that I had said or believed. She also prayed against fears and other related issues, and she prayed life, peace, joy and healing over me. She encouraged me to continue to do "soakings," on my own and also with other friends and family members. Finally, after speaking to me over a period of several months, she realised that for the Lord to be able to minister into my deep fears and traumas, and because of the huge deficit of touch and human affection in my life, I needed to find one or two trustworthy women with a heart for broken people. These women should sit with me, hold me and pray with me, while listening to worship music. I would receive in my spirit from the music, while their touch and prayers would minister to my damaged emotions. It proved very difficult to find anyone who was able and willing to do this with me. However, my friend Lily agreed to try to do this with me, and we continued over a period of time. I began to gain a sense of worth, and grew in confidence. After a time, due to personal circumstances, Lily was unable to continue to help me in this way. However she has remained a good solid friend. Over the next two years, our family made several further visits to conferences at the church near Birmingham. On one such visit, one of the speakers was an Indian lady. As she ministered God's word and testimony, the love of God was powerfully manifested. After speaking, she was willing to hold me in her arms as I lay on the floor, allowing the Holy Spirit to minister into my heart. She held me in this way for about an hour, speaking words of comfort to my soul and spirit. This hour of ministry had a profoundly helpful effect on me. When I got back home, I continued to look for opportunities to soak in God's presence. I started meeting up with Sylvia once a month. Sometimes we would meet for a coffee and a chat, and sometimes we would have a time of soaking prayer together.

After a few years break, I started to work again as a lunchtime supervisory assistant. I was now feeling stronger and more confident. Soon I felt that I could do more than this job of only an hour a day. I decided to put myself forward for training as a "School Escort." This involves work with disabled children, accompanying one or more children in a taxi from their homes to their place of education, and back again. I successfully completed the training and was employed. I have gained both enjoyment and satisfaction from doing this work.

Over the last year or two I have also attended the nearby "Healing Rooms", from time to time. I found that the volunteers, who are from different churches, were always very loving and supportive, both to me and to my family members. They spend time in prayer before seeing each person, asking God for a Bible verse, a picture or direction, and I have personally found their ministry encouraging and up building.

Perhaps the most important thing, which has helped me get through life over the years, is my love for Jesus, and of course, His love for me. Because of this, I have been able to go back to places where I have been hurt and wounded, even though my feelings and emotions were telling me to give up on a church or even on the Christian life. Realising that the enemy of our souls is out to kill and destroy, I would do my best to say "no" to these negative feelings, as I always knew deep in my heart that Jesus was with me. I believed what it said in his Word. Even though a church might forsake me, Jesus would never leave me nor forsake me. Because of this, I was able to stand up against the negative feelings, and push on through. I have always continued to pray. I pray every day while walking in the woods or near the river with my dog, Sam. I like to do this in the mornings, which prepares me for the day ahead. I have seen results from some of my prayers, which helps me know that God listens and answers prayer.

As I close this account of my life to-date, the Lord has recently led my family and I to a caring and lively church, where the leaders and the people have welcomed us and have accepted us for who we are. They believe that every member of the Body of Christ is needed and important, and that healing, miracles, prophecy and all the gifts of the Spirit are as relevant today as they were in Bible times. They are keen to help us with prayer and ministry, as well as human friendship and fellowship, and see us move forward into a deeper and more intimate walk with the Father, Jesus and Holy Spirit.

"Epilogue"

It has taken a long time for God to bring me to this place, where I am now, as I complete this book. Yet I feel that this is really only just the beginning for me. I know He still has much more yet to do in my life and for my family. Above all, *I also know that He is faithful* – so much more faithful to us than we are to him! My desire is to bring hope and healing to others who have suffered and struggled in life, like me. I hope soon to be able to speak and minister the love of Jesus to others. Who knows, maybe you will be one of them!

Finally, my daughter has written a little poem for me, which has relevance for my life and also to this book. I would like to take the opportunity to end with it.

"Hope"

Hope, like the sun rising, dispelling the dark,
A ray of light to a weary heart,
With joy and peace, she walks hand in hand
Bringing life into broken dreams.

A voice that is sweet will whisper in your ear
It says, "Do not despair for your hope is here,"
She will lead you by the hand to the river of life
Where freedom and joy will prevail.

Acknowledgements

I would like to give my acknowledgement and sincere thanks to the people who have helped and encouraged me in my walk with the Lord, and in writing this book.

I would like to give my heartfelt thanks to Sandy and Luther for standing with me and supporting me over many years. I would also like to thank Liz, Arthur and Maro, Frank and Hazel, Lily, David and Diana, Steve L, Sylvia, Gay, Val, Steve and Sue, Miriam, and Faith. Also Estelle, Fiona, and Donna at "The Bridge" and Claire, Maggi, Sandra and Richard at the "Healing Rooms." My heartfelt thanks go to you all for your help, prayers and support and for being part of my life. I appreciate it very much.

I would like to say a big thank you to Paul and Toni, for their help in editing this book and for encouraging me to write it. Also, my sincere thanks and blessings to everyone who has helped me in my life, and who has not been personally mentioned in this book. Finally, many thanks also to my husband, Bruce, for helping me with the writing of this book.

Printed in the United Kingdom by
Lightning Source UK Ltd., Milton Keynes
140079UK00001B/4/P

9 781906 645953